BEFORE ALPHA

BEFORE ALPHA

Learning Games for the Under Fives

BEVÉ HORNSBY

Drawings by
Julia and Justina Hornsby

SOUVENIR PRESS

ACKNOWLEDGEMENTS

The author would like to thank the following for granting permission to use copyright material:

W. W. Norton & Company, Inc., New York, for permission to quote from *The Mismeasure of Man* by S. J. Gould (1981); and the United Kingdom Reading Association for permission to reproduce a table from 'Follow-up of educational attainment in a group of children with retarded speech development and in a control group' by A. W. Mason, in the *UKR Proceedings, Reading: Influences on Progress*, edited by Margaret M. Clark and Sheila M. Maxwell (1969), pp. 37–44.

CONTENTS

INTRODUCTION

Before Alpha is a carefully structured programme which develops the skills a child needs to acquire in preparation for formal education. It is intended to be used by parents, nursery and primary school teachers, speech therapists or anyone concerned with enriching the minds of young children. Each session is designed to build and expand on the concepts taught in the previous one. The programme should therefore be followed logically and in the order in which it appears in the book, but there is no time limit on when it should be completed, and children can progress through it at their own pace.

If the sessions are given on a daily basis, you may only need to spend two days on each one. On the other hand, some children may require a week on each session, which can then be speeded up as they begin to grasp what is required of them.

The rate at which you work through the programme depends, therefore, on how quickly the individual children learn, but you will find that the intellectual stimulation provided by the sessions will gradually increase the speed at which new concepts can be absorbed and retained, so increasing the child's rate of progress.

Before they can learn to read and write, children must master the following skills:

Visual perception and discrimination
    Visual sequencing
    Visual categorisation
    Visual memory
Auditory perception and discrimination
    Auditory sequencing
    Auditory categorisation
    Auditory memory
Manual dexterity for fine motor control
Appreciation of the relationship between shapes
Knowledge of left and right, up and down, backwards and forwards
Knowledge of colour
Knowledge of number
Full spoken language competence, such as:
    Correct use of tense and concord
    Correct use of pronouns

Correct sentence construction
Ability to follow instructions and to organise thoughts so that
instructions can be given

Only when all these skills have been mastered can the child
proceed to a knowledge of the alphabet on which written language
is based.

As you work through the programme, you will become aware of
any areas in which a child needs extra help, so that by the time you
have completed all the sessions, every child should be proficient in
each of the skills listed above. The programme is therefore an aid
not only to teaching children, but also to diagnosing their particular
problems.

HOW CHILDREN ACQUIRE LANGUAGE

Children begin to acquire language soon after birth—in their mothers' arms. This is where they learn to associate the pleasurable sensations of 'food-warmth-comfort' with the human voice—the mother's voice. All the sounds that are most important to them come from close by, and are linked in their minds to the gratification of their needs. This pleasurable association prompts them to try out sounds for themselves, and from the pleasure of this achievement comes the urge to imitate themselves (babbling). Then they realise that they can extend this exercise and imitate others (lalling or echolalia), and that others will imitate them—and so the pleasure of verbal communication is born.

The next stage is the association of the objects or persons in the child's environment with specific labels—the first words with meaning—and the first one of all is usually 'mama', since the first link in the chain was forged with her. Occasionally it is 'nana' or 'dada', and one can draw one's own conclusions from this! Thereafter the naming process gradually expands to other objects and persons in the infant's immediate circle—milk, cup, drink, 'gaga', etc.—and then further afield. Nouns and verbs (the content words) come first, because these are the words which carry the most meaning; then the functional words, articles, prepositions, conjunctions, etc.—in other words, those which one would leave out in a telegram, hence the term 'the telegrammatic speech of the young child'. Finally, syntax and grammar are acquired (use of plurals, tenses, concepts of causality, number and colour, etc.), until, by the age of five, language acquisition is complete. After this it merely becomes more sophisticated.

It does not take much imagination to realise that if any of the links in the chain are broken, the acquisition of language is likely to be inhibited or disturbed.

I am not suggesting that all children with retarded language development have had an unsatisfactory mother/child relationship, or other trauma in their young lives: in fact, in nine cases out of ten, some physical/neurological reasons are indicated. Nevertheless, one must bear in mind that, had such conditions existed, they might have played some part. More important, however, when one is endeavouring to teach language to a child with delayed language development, is to have a very clear picture of this natural progression from the first seed to the final flowering, and to follow its course in one's remedial treatment. It is very little use to exhort a non-speaking child to 'say this' and 'say that' when one has not even made the first link of associating pleasurable experience with verbalisation. Never try to jump the gun and begin at the end—it cannot possibly work. Each step must be religiously worked through, and progression to the next step must follow logically from the last.

Helping Your Child at Home

Use all the experiences in your child's life which you know give him pleasure, and supply him with the words he does not have to name these things, using only nouns to begin with. For example, name the foods you are giving him, and the objects he is using—spoon, fork, cup, etc.—and when going for a walk, name the things you see that you think might interest him. Bath time should be pleasurable, so name the things associated with this. All naming should be done in context, with the actual objects there in front of his eyes. At bed-time, look at picture books, naming the things you have been seeing and doing during the day, preferably cuddling him in your arms at the same time, so that the original situation is reproduced as far as possible. It is said that a normal child needs approximately 600 repetitions before he associates an object with its label. The rate of input must also be slow and simple if he is to take it in—in other words, always speak very slowly, clearly and simply.

Listening activities should be encouraged—again preferably sitting on your lap. Provide him with plenty of occupation and cut down on situations that cause frustration. Boredom and frustration nearly always lead to behaviour problems.

Reading starts with nursery rhymes, where the child learns to enjoy the rhythm and rhyming of words without bothering too much about meaning. Have him participate by looking at the pictures and finishing the last word of the rhyme.

Finger play rhymes come next, when the child learns to integrate the senses of sight, hearing, touch and movement. Here he becomes more of a participant—almost an equal one, especially if they are repeated often enough for him to be able to say the rhyme with you while doing the actions.

Next, move on to longer stories like *Goldilocks and the Three Bears*, with a recurring phrase pattern so that the child can join in; these are also excellent for accompanying gestures, and for giving experience of voice pitch changes—low for father, medium for mother, high for baby—as well as for comparison of adjectives:

    too high, too low, too wide, just right
    too hard, too soft, just right
    too big, medium-sized, teeny-weeny
    too hot, too cold, just right

All these comparisons should be illustrated by gesture and facial expression, so that even such abstract concepts as sad, happy and frightened can be understood.

Throughout this book, for the sake of simplicity, I refer to 'the teacher', but this could equally refer to 'the parent' or 'the therapist'. Similarly, the gender 'he' has been adopted for 'the child' to avoid the tiresome he/she distinction. In this case, therefore, 'he' is 'unisex'.

Finally, try to relax and not be too worried or anxious if your child does not immediately respond—or at least, do not show it. Anxiety very soon rubs off on to the child, and may set up undesirable reactions. Always give praise, even for small achievements.

The programme was originally devised as a one-year course for use with children with delayed language development. The age range was five to six years and a control study was undertaken by giving the Reynell Developmental Scales at the beginning of the year and repeating them at the end. If the children's progress had only kept pace with the clock—that is, they had only made one year's progress in one year of time—it would have been assumed that the programme had not accelerated their language acquisition and that such a programme was unnecessary and by implication ineffective. In fact, the results were so encouraging that the programme has subsequently been used with great success both with small groups and individuals with a variety of problems, and also with younger children without specific difficulties, in order to stimulate language and intellectual growth.

TABLE I

No. of children	Age range	Average rate of progress
6	5–6 yrs	2½ years in 1 year of treatment

It has long been realised that speech and language development are strongly related to the later acquisition of written language skills. In a subsequent study, children whose speech and language were retarded were compared with a group of children with normal language development. The following results were observed:

TABLE II

A *Reading retardation (6 months below chronological age, irrespective of intellectual level)*
Speech retarded   15 of 51 children   29%
Normal control   1 of 78 children   1%

B *Spelling retardation*
Speech retarded   18 of 51 children   35%
Normal control   5 of 78 children   6%

C *Arithmetic retardation*
Speech retarded   4 of 51 children   8%
Normal control   6 of 78 children   8%

From Mason (1960)

Only reading and spelling were affected by the late speech and language development: arithmetic achievement was at the same level in both groups.

These findings appear to agree with Dr Ian Macfarlane Smith's view that arithmetic ability is closely associated with spatial ability, which is the hemispheric opposite of verbal ability.

Rawson (1968) states that reading skill is only one part of language development and depends on established skills in recognition and production of spoken language, which are all aspects of the decoding and encoding needed for the management of the symbolic communication of ideas.

Working on the assumption, then, that four types of skill need to be present and functioning adequately for language (both spoken and written) to develop normally, the activities devised for the Before Alpha programme aim to train these skills and their interrelationships with one another. The types of skill are:

a   Motor skills, both fine and gross.
b   Visual perception and memory.
c   Auditory perception and memory.
d   Social skills and relationships.

Each session contains activities to promote the development of these skills. There has been some controversy about whether it is better to utilise a child's assets or to train his deficits, but the difference would seem to be more apparent than real for it is not an either/or question. It is necessary to use the assets *and* to train the deficits. Current thinking does not hold that deficits are innate and unalterable (Kirk, 1971); if they were, one would, of course, have to rely entirely on assets. Assuming that most learning disabilities can be improved, I believe that one should try to develop abilities which are not functioning adequately, disregarding a deficit and developing other abilities to take its place in compensation—this may be necessary in certain cases, where a particular skill is severely affected.

The Before Alpha programme is therefore a multisensory one, using more than one type of skill as initial stimulus. For example, in the game of 'Simon says', the teacher at first offers the visual stimulus at the same time as the auditory one, by wiggling her fingers as she says, 'Simon says wiggle your fingers.' Later the visual clue is withdrawn and the teacher simply says, 'Simon says wiggle your fingers.' In this situation the child learns to follow the auditory command without visual clues for imitation. He has learned to 'hear and do', that is, he has learned to interpret what he hears in order to perform the action (auditory-motor encoding).

On the formal language side the programme aims to take the children from simple naming of objects and the demonstration of their use, through to more complex concepts such as comparison of adjectives, similarities and differences in objects and the concept of cause and effect.

Activities in the first stage are chosen so that they will have a dual role at a later date. Thus, listening to the story *Goldilocks and the Three Bears*, designed to develop a listening attitude in the first instance, will have implications later in the programme when comparison of objects is reached (big, medium sized, little; hard, soft, just right; too hot, too cold, etc.).

The final objectives are:

Being able to relate two abstract concepts such as happy–sad, fast–slow, like–dislike, good–bad, etc.

Correct use of all pronouns, including his, hers, theirs, etc.

Correct use of all prepositions, including between, behind, beside, near, etc.

Correct identification of right and left hands and feet.

Correct identification and naming of 12 colours.

Correct use of the number concept up to ten.

Correct use of sentences—no words omitted.

Correct use of plurals, including some common irregular ones such as 'mice'.

Correct classification and categorisation of common groups of objects such as toys, colours, transport, fruit, vegetables.

Correct knowledge of parts of the body, including more obscure ones such as elbows, eyebrows, knees, etc.

Correct use of the 'not' concept—that is, being able to state what things are *not*, as well as 'what they are'.

Being able to supply a rhyming word, such as 'I have a cat, her name is Able, she is sitting under the . . . ?'

Being able to beat or clap in time to a simple rhythm.

Being able to interpret musical moods—fast, slow, quiet, etc.

If the children attend for only one hourly session per week, it is particularly important that parents and teachers should work together, so that the lessons of one session may be kept in mind until the next. The parents should therefore be encouraged to watch and listen, explanatory talks should be given from time to time, and suggestions for home activities should be made available. Copies should be made of all rhymes, songs and stories used in the sessions, and these given to the parents so that they can be practised at home. If the programme is used on a daily basis, however, this may not be necessary.

All the equipment used should be found in any reasonably well equipped speech therapy clinic or nursery school, and many of the games can be made at home at very little cost.

Although the sessions are structured from beginning to end, no opportunity should be missed for having a discussion which might arise from the children's remarks. Spontaneous conversation should be encouraged and expanded at all times.

The children should be seated at a low table with small chairs, so that their feet rest comfortably on the floor, and most activities, with the exception of the closing activities, are conducted sitting at the table. The object of keeping the children seated and of structuring the session to allow for very little free activity, is to train them in concentration and attention. A lot of children are hyperactive and have a very short concentration span, and part of their learning difficulties stem from their inability to attend. It is astonishing to note the accelerated progress made once this distractibility has been overcome.

In spite of the fact that the programme was developed with the language delayed child in mind, it has become increasingly clear over the years that early education of this kind can produce startling results with all children. There have been two slightly contradictory view-points expressed: Walmsley and Margolis (1978) in *Hot House People* suggest that intensive early education can produce children with exceptional abilities, while other educationalists and psychologists firmly believe that intelligence is innate and immutable. The truth lies somewhere between the two, but 'few tragedies can be more extensive than the stunting of life, few injustices deeper than the denial of an opportunity to strive or even to hope, by a limit imposed from without but falsely identified as lying within,' as Stephen Jay Gould says in *The Mismeasure of Man*.

A number of would-be enrichers of children's lives have found to their cost that a simple faith in a benign physical environment is no substitute for genuinely effective educational interventions. There is now a substantial body of empirical evidence pointing firmly to the conclusion that for most if not all children, with careful and imaginative use of the resources that are available to parents, teachers and therapists, the scope for increased and accelerated early progress is truly enormous. Research findings provide strong grounds for arguing that it is definitely within the means of any literate parents (as well as professionals) who are able to make fairly substantial investments of time, planning, care and patience, to give their children the kind of early start in life that will vastly increase any individual's chances of becoming an outstandingly able young person (Bloom, 1985; Fowler, 1983; Howe, 1982). Remember, though, that the art of teaching the young lies in presenting material in concrete forms—do not present abstractions familiar to ourselves to minds unprepared for them.

References

BEREITER, C., and ENGELMANN, S. (1966). *Teaching Disadvantaged Children in the Pre-School*. New Jersey: Prentice-Hall, Inc.

BLOOM, B. S. (ed.) (1985). *Developing Talent in Young People*. New York: Ballantine.

FOWLER, W. (1981). 'Case studies of cognitive precocity; the rôle of exogenous and endogenous stimulation in early mental development'. In *Journal of Applied Developmental Psychology*, 2, 319–367.

GESELL, A. (ed.) (1971). *The First Five Years Of Life*. London: Methuen.

GETMAN, G. L. *et al.* (1968). *Developing Learning Readiness*. Manchester, Mo: McGraw-Hill.

GOODENOUGH, F. (1962). 'Draw a Man Test'. In F. Goodenough, *The Measurement of Intelligence by Drawings*. New York: World Books.

GOULD, S. J. (1981). *The Mismeasure of Man*. New York: Norton.

HOWE, M. J. A. (1982). 'Biographical evidence in the development of outstanding individuals'. In *American Psychologist*, 37, 1071–1081.

INGRAM, T. T. S. (1963). 'Delayed Development of Speech, with special reference to Dyslexia'. In *Proceedings of the Royal Society of Medicine*, 56, 199.

ISAACS, S. (1951). *Intellectual Growth in Young Children*. Humanities Press.

KARNES, M. B. *et al.* (1968). 'Activities for developing psycholinguistic skills with preschool culturally disadvantaged children'. Washington DC. Council for exceptional children.

KIRK, S. A., and KIRK, W. D. (1971). *Psycholinguistic Learning Disabilities: diagnosis and remediation*. University of Illinois Press.

MASON, A. W. (1960). 'Follow-up of educational attainment in a group of children with retarded speech development and in a control group'. Paper given to the United Kingdom Reading Association, Edinburgh: August 1968.

RAWSON, M. B. (1968). *Developmental Language Disability: Adult*

Accomplishment of Dyslexic Boys. Baltimore: Johns Hopkins Press.

REYNELL, J. (1971). *The Development Language Scales.* Windsor: NFER–Nelson Publishing Co.

SHERIDAN, M. D. (1969). *The Development Progress of Infants and Young Children.* London: Her Majesty's Stationery Office.

SHERIDAN, M. D. (1964). 'Development of Auditory attention and language symbols in young children'. In C. Renfew and K. Murphy (eds), *The Child who does not Talk.* Clinics in Development Medicine. London: Heinemann.

SMITH, I. M. (1964). *Spatial Ability.* University of London Press.

WALMSLEY, J., and Margolis, J. (1987). *Hot House People: Can we create super Human Beings?* London: Pan Books.

THE
BEFORE ALPHA
PROGRAMME

STAGE ONE
SESSION I

Materials required
Mosaic pattern-making kit.
Percussion instruments—bells, triangle, tambourine, maracas, drum, whistle.
Small tins containing different ingredients: salt, small stones, pins, rice, buttons, wooden beads. Tobacco tins make excellent containers.
Six toy farm animals, one for each child: cow, horse, pig, sheep, hen, duck.
Six cards with pictures of objects with a final 't' sound. These can be made from Philip & Tacy's picture stamps which can be stuck onto cards.
Picture lotto.
Music tapes for musical bumps.

Concepts taught
Visual Perception—copying patterns.
Rhythm—beating time with musical instruments.
Auditory Perception—different contents to be identified.
Preposition—under.
Identifying farm animals, their uses and their sounds. Final 't' for articulation practice.
Singing—nursery rhyme, *Baa Baa Black Sheep*.
Picture lotto—with objects ending in 'p', 'b', 't', or 'd' (for correct pronunciation only).
Integrating speech with actions—finger play rhyme, *Ten Little Men*.
Listening—*Goldilocks and the Three Bears*, appreciating comparisons of size and feelings through use of adjectives: too big, too small, too hot, too cold, angry, frightened, and so on.
Acting—playing at being milkman, dustman, etc., and simple number work.
Activity—musical bumps.
Finale—social awareness, plus reinforcement of prepositions of position.

1   Opening Activity—Visual Perception
Copying patterns displayed on cards with mosaic pins and pin boards (or can just as well be done with felt shapes and felt boards).

2   Rhythm

Each child is given an instrument: bells, triangle, drum, tambourine, maracas, whistle. They shake or beat them in time to the conducting of the teacher. Then she beats a short rhythm on the table and each child in turn copies it with his instrument.

3   Basic Ear Training

Using the tins containing the different ingredients, give them to the children asking them to guess what might be in them. When the contents and the sounds associated with them are fully understood, the teacher takes the tins and shakes them under the table one at a time. The children try to guess which tin is being shaken.

4   Use of Prepositions
—'under'

Using six farm animals—cow, horse, pig, sheep, hen, duck—first elicit from the children the names of the animals and incorporate further ear training by giving them correct and incorrect articulation patterns. Discuss to what uses these animals can be put and where one is likely to find them. Ask what they say. Then the teacher says the sound and the children call out the name of the animal. Next present six cards (one at a time) of objects having a final 't' sound, such as cat, hat, mat, bat, net, kite. Elicit the names and correct articulation by ear training as before. Explain that these animals and the pictures on the cards are names of things and are called nouns; names and nouns both begin with the sound 'n'. Taking each child in turn, ask him to place a card 'under' one of the farm animals. When all cards have been placed ask the child to hand you the (cat, bat, etc.) and to say where he found it. Full sentences must be elicited.

5   Singing

Baa baa black sheep, have you any wool?
Yes sir, yes sir, three bags full,
One for the master, one for the dame,
And one for the little boy who lives down the lane.

6   Picture Lotto

Played like Bingo. First lotto should have objects which have 'p', 'b', 't' or 'd' for their final sounds. When child identifies the picture shown, with the picture on his card he says, 'I have a cat' (or whatever the picture happens to be). He thus learns to use the correct pronoun and the indefinite article, as well as having further practice in visual perception, and articulation of final 't'.

7 Associating Speech with Actions—Finger Play Rhyme
Ten little men standing up straight
(Hold up both hands with fingers straight)
Ten little men open the gate
(Open all fingers)
Ten little men make a big ring
(Join thumbs and little fingers to make a ring)
Ten little men bow to the king
(Bow hands down to table)
Ten little men running to play
(Run fingers all over table)
Ten little men hiding away
(Hide hands behind back).

8 Listening Activity
Read the story of *Goldilocks and the Three Bears*, using gesture for comparison of size, feelings, adjectives—associating listening with doing. Later the children will act the parts.

GOLDILOCKS AND THE THREE BEARS

Once upon a time there was a little girl named Goldilocks. She was called Goldilocks because she had beautiful golden hair. One day, when Goldilocks was walking through the woods, she saw a dear little house. The door was open, so Goldilocks walked in to see who lived there. There was no one at home, but in the living room she saw three chairs—a great big chair, a middle-sized chair and a tiny weeny chair. Goldilocks tried to sit in the great big chair, but it was too high. Next she tried to sit in the middle-sized chair, but it was too wide. Then she sat down on the tiny weeny chair, and it was just right. But suddenly the bottom of the chair fell out and down she went, plop, on the floor.

Then Goldilocks went into the dining room, and there she saw three bowls of porridge on the table—a great big bowl, a middle-sized bowl and a tiny weeny bowl. She tasted the porridge in the great big bowl, but it was too hot. Next she tasted the porridge in the middle-sized bowl, but it was too cold. Then she tasted the porridge in the tiny weeny bowl, and it was just right, so she gobbled it all up. Then Goldilocks went upstairs, and there she saw three beds—a great big bed, a middle-sized bed and a tiny weeny bed. She tried the great big bed, but it was too hard. Next she tried the middle-sized bed, but it was too soft. Then she tried the tiny weeny bed, and it was just right. Soon she was fast asleep.

Now about this time, the three bears who lived in this house came home. There was a great big Daddy bear, a middle-sized Mummy bear, and a tiny weeny Baby bear. They had been taking a walk in the woods while they waited for their porridge to cool. As soon as they came into the house Daddy bear said, 'Who has been sitting in my chair?' and Mummy bear said, 'Who has been sitting in my chair?' and Baby bear said, 'Who has been sitting in my chair, and broken it all to pieces?' Then he cried and cried.

Next, the three bears went into the dining room. Right away Daddy bear said, 'Who has been tasting my porridge?' Mummy bear said, 'Who has been tasting my porridge?' Baby bear stood on tiptoes and looked in his bowl. 'Who has been tasting my porridge and eaten it all up?' Then he cried and cried.

Next, the three bears went upstairs, and Daddy bear said, 'Who has been lying on my bed?' Mummy bear said, 'Who has been lying on my bed?' Baby bear squealed, 'Oh, look who's lying on my bed right now.' When Baby bear squealed Goldilocks woke up. She was so surprised to see three bears looking at her that she jumped out of the bed and then out of the window. She ran all the way home. You can be sure she never went into any house again without permission.

9   Acting
Being:
    milkman
    dustman
    postman
    baker
incorporating number work by asking child to deliver (or bake) a given number of objects, up to three.

10   Musical Bumps
Play this by all joining hands in a circle and dancing round until the music stops when everyone sits on the floor—the last one being called 'donkey'. Joining hands brings in the shy, withdrawn children who are not good at joining in with these activities. Do not make the last child to sit down be 'out', as this often leads to distress.

Finale
Line up to receive two Smarties [raisins] each, asking children to arrange themselves in given positions—i.e. John stand 'between' Jane and Bill, Jennifer 'next' to Colin, etc.

    Shake hands and say Goodbye and Thank you.

Materials required
Plasticine.
Mosaics.
Tins of materials as before, but two tins now required which have
the same contents, e.g. two tins of rice, two tins of small stones,
two tins of salt, two tins of pins, two tins of wooden beads, two
tins of buttons.
Set of stacking coloured boxes.
Cards of objects, ending in the sound 'p'.
Picture lotto of verbs.
Hand puppet.
Tape recording of *Goldilocks and the Three Bears* with male voice.

Concepts taught
Manual dexterity—plasticine modelling.
Visual sequencing and orientation—copying series of shapes.
Ear training—'same' or 'different', using tins of 'same' or 'different'
materials.
Prepositions—'in', 'on', 'under'.
Identifying objects with final 'p' but extending the concept to
incorporate 'similarities' and long and short vowels.
Singing—*Baa Baa Black Sheep*.
Verbs—picture lotto.
Finger play—*Ten Little Men*.
Acting—'Simon says', using parts of the body.
Auditory memory—listening and attention, tape recording of
Goldilocks and the Three Bears.
Activity—musical bumps.
Finale—social awareness, plus reinforcement of prepositions of
position.

1 Opening Activity—Manual Dexterity
Plasticine. Show each child how to roll long thin sausages of
plasticine between his hand and the table. These sausages can then
be formed into baskets, snakes, people, animals, etc.

2 Visual Sequencing and Orientation
The children are asked to copy a series of shapes arranged by the

teacher with the mosaics, ensuring that the child not only arranges the shapes in the correct order, but the right way up. Use the following shapes to begin with—circle, square, triangle, working up to diamond, oblong and hexagon in later sessions.

3   Basic Ear Training

With tins, some filled with the same material and some with different material. Children to say which sounds are the same and which different, when shaken by the teacher. Begin with easy choices such as stones versus salt, beads versus pins. Then decrease the difference so that the sounds become more and more similar.

4   Use of Prepositions

— 'in', 'on', 'under'

Use a set of coloured stacking boxes, some arranged lying on their sides, some with open end uppermost and some with open end on the table. Present six cards as before but with objects that have a *final 'p'* sound, and proceed with the same routine as in Session I, that is, discussing what the objects on the cards are and any similarities they might have—e.g. 'cap' and 'cape' are both clothing; 'ape' and 'pup' are both animals; 'cup' and 'soup' are both to do with drinking. Then, using the prepositions 'in', 'on' or 'under', ask each child to place his card 'in', 'on' or 'under' one of the boxes. He must choose which box he can put a card 'in' and which 'on'. Clearly, 'under' will not require the choice of a box with open side up or down, as either will do.

   Then ask each child to give you his card, saying where he found it, e.g. 'The cup was under the red box.' If the child cannot manage this spontaneously, say the sentence and have the child repeat it.

5   Singing

Baa baa black sheep, have you any wool?
Yes sir, yes sir, three bags full,
One for the master, one for the dame,
And one for the little boy who lives down the lane.

6   Picture Lotto

Illustrating verbs, i.e. running, sitting, climbing, walking, standing, catching, throwing, etc. The child must say, as before, 'I have a girl running,' 'I have a boy sitting,' and so on.

   If the child has difficulty producing the appropriate sentence, say it for him, and have him repeat it after you.

7   **Finger Play**

> Ten little men standing up straight
> *(Hold up both hands with fingers straight)*
> Ten little men open the gate
> *(Open all fingers)*
> Ten little men make a big ring
> *(Join thumbs and little fingers to make a ring)*
> Ten little men bow to the King
> *(Bow hands down to table)*
> Ten little men running to play
> *(Run fingers all over table)*
> Ten little men hiding away
> *(Hide hands behind back).*

8   **Acting Game**

Following directions, and gaining knowledge of parts of the body.

To aid attention, use a hand puppet to supposedly give the directions. Say:

> 'Simon says: Close your eyes
>   Open your eyes
>   Touch your mouth
>   Pull your ears
>   Pat your head
>   Raise one arm
>   Raise both arms
>   Put your hands behind your back
>   Stand up
>   Stand on one foot
>   Stand on your toes
>   Sit down.'

The children should follow the instructions, but you may demonstrate if they are having difficulty.

9   **Auditory Memory—Listening and Attention**

Story—*Goldilocks and the Three Bears* (see p. 25), previously recorded (preferably a male voice with a range of pitch changes for the three bears) on a tape recorder. In this session everyone merely listens quietly to the story.

10   **Musical Bumps**

As for Session I.

Finale

A final line-up to receive Smarties, with positioning of the children as before. Shake hands and say Goodbye and Thank you.

Materials required

Galt or Abbatt wooden puzzles, 3–5 year level.

Six small objects on a tray or lid of a box.

Matchbox toys of different forms of transport.

Six cards with pictures of objects ending in 'n' or 'm'.

Picture lotto with two objects on the Bingo cards and a single of the same object on the pack of cards the teacher turns over. (See example below.)

Tape recording of *Goldilocks and the Three Bears* with male voice.

Toy domestic animals.

Bingo card might look like this:

Teacher's cards will be:

Concepts taught

Visual perception, spatial awareness plus manual dexterity—puzzles.

Visual memory—'what's missing?'

Singing—*Baa Baa Black Sheep, Polly Put the Kettle On*.

Use of prepositions 'in', 'on', 'under', 'in front of', 'behind'.

Transport.

Gesture.

Picture lotto—plurals.

Auditory memory and gesture.
Vocabulary building.
Activity—musical bumps.
The Farmer's in his Den.
Finale—social awareness, plus reinforcement of prepositions of
  position.

1   Opening Activity—Visual Perception, Spatial Awareness plus Manual Dexterity

Puzzles—lay out one wooden puzzle for each child. As the children
finish one puzzle, they can exchange with another child who has
also finished, so that each child has the opportunity to do two or
three puzzles. Helpful suggestions can be given to those children
who have difficulty, but then give the child time to work it out for
himself.

2   Visual Memory

'What's missing?' Place six objects on a tray (or lid of a box), ask the
children to look carefully and try to remember what is there.
Remove the tray out of sight of the children and remove one of the
objects. Return the tray to the table and ask the children to say what
is missing. Repeat until all objects have had a turn at being removed.

3   Singing

Baa baa black sheep, have you any wool?
Yes sir, yes sir, three bags full,
One for the master, one for the dame,
And one for the little boy who lives down the lane.

Polly put the kettle on,
Polly put the kettle on,
Polly put the kettle on,
We'll all have tea.
Suky take it off again,
Suky take it off again,
Suky take it off again,
They've all gone away.

4   Use of Prepositions

—'in', 'on', 'under', 'in front of', 'behind'
Using Matchbox toys: forms of transport. Bus, fire engine, ambulance,

pick-up lorry, motor bike, helicopter. Name and discuss them; then present six cards with objects having final 'm' or 'n'. Proceed as before. Then conduct an auditory discrimination exercise by asking each child whether the object you show him ends in 'n' or 'm'.

5   Recognition of Gesture
'What am I doing?' Teacher mimes the following, asking children to guess what she is doing:
   brushing hair
   cleaning
   knitting
   threading needle
   smoking
   drinking
   eating
   sleeping
   yawning
   talking on telephone
Now ask the children in turn to mime these actions.

6   Picture Lotto/Bingo
Use pictures depicting the use of simple plurals. Teacher turns over her card saying, 'I have one cat. Who has two . . . . ?' Child has to supply the word with the added 's' if the picture is on his card.

7   Auditory Memory, Listening and Attention plus Gesture
Listen to the story *Goldilocks and the Three Bears* (see p. 25) on the tape recorder, but this time the children make appropriate gestures wherever possible. The teacher can also make the gestures so that the children can copy, as they may still not be able to do this on their own.

8   Vocabulary Building plus Classification plus Vocalisation
Naming *domestic* animals (found in the home or on a farm) from memory—animals are then produced from a box as they are called out, then everyone tries to make the noise the animal makes.

Suggestions:
bee says buzz buzz
cat says meow meow
cow says moo moo
dog says bow wow
donkey says he haw
duck says quack quack

pig says oink oink
cock says cock a doodle doo
sheep says baa baa

Children must then separate them into those found in the home and those on a farm.

9 Musical Bumps
Played as before.

10 The Farmer's in his Den
With the children singing as they act it out. The children form a ring and hold hands, and dance round singing while one child is chosen to be the farmer and stands in the middle of the ring.

The farmer's in his den,
The farmer's in his den,
Hey ho diddly oh,
The farmer's in his den.
The farmer wants a wife,
The farmer wants a wife.
Hey ho diddly oh,
The farmer wants a wife.
(The child in the middle then chooses another child to be his wife.)
The wife wants a child,
The wife wants a child,
Hey ho diddly oh,
The wife wants a child.
(The 'wife' then chooses another child to be the 'child'.)
The child wants a nurse,
The child wants a nurse,
Hey ho diddly oh,
The child wants a nurse.
(The child then chooses a 'nurse'.)
The nurse wants a dog,
The nurse wants a dog,
Hey ho diddly oh,
The nurse wants a dog.
(The nurse then chooses a 'dog'.)
The dog wants a bone,
The dog wants a bone,
Hey ho diddly oh,
The dog wants a bone.
(The dog chooses a child to be the 'bone'.)

We all pat the dog,
We all pat the dog,
Hey ho diddly oh,
We all pat the dog.
(All the children pat the child who is the 'dog'.)

Finale
Line up for Smarties, following instructions: Peter stand behind
Joan, Jean stand in front of Tom, etc.
    Shake hands and say Goodbye and Thank you.

Materials required
Coloured wooden blocks 2.5 cms (1 inch) square.
Doll's house furniture with figures of man, woman, one boy, two girls and a baby.
Pack of six cards with pictures of objects with a final 'b' and 'd' sound.
Fairground picture, or any large colourful pictures with plenty of action in them. Postcards of paintings by famous artists provide useful material.

Concepts taught
Eye-hand co-ordination—towers of cubes.
Vocabulary building—doll's house furniture.
Prepositions 'in', 'on', 'under', 'in front of', 'behind', 'between'.
Auditory discrimination—final 'b' and 'd'.
Following instructions.
Animal noises.
Auditory decoding—true or false?
Appreciation of rhyme and rhythm.
Singing—*Polly Put the Kettle On.*
Left, right discrimination—*I am a Teapot.*
Descriptive ability—fairground picture.
Motor encoding—musical bumps
Finale—social awareness, plus reinforcement of prepositions of position.

1   Opening Activity—Eye-hand Co-ordination
Building towers with coloured cubes, also copying steps with six cubes and bridge with three cubes. (See p. 36.) Record each child's achievements and see Appendix for norms for these activities.

2   Vocabulary Building and Use of Prepositions
—'in', 'on', 'under', 'in front of', 'behind', 'between'.
—ear training for final 'b' and 'd' sounds in words.
Using the doll's house furniture, have each child decide which room in the house he is going to collect and then ask him to select the appropriate items for his choice, naming each one as he does so:
  sitting room

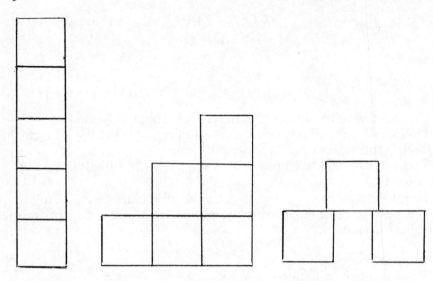

bedroom
kitchen
bathroom
dining room
nursery

When each child has his room, discuss what one does in each room. Then give each child a figure and ask where each figure would be *most likely* to be found. If the child puts the father in the kitchen it would be interesting to ask why this choice was made and to discuss the reply with the other children.

Now turn over the pack of six picture cards ending in 'b' or 'd', one at a time, asking each child to name the object and to say whether the word ends in 'b' or 'd'.

The child is then asked to put his card in, on, under, in front of, behind or between one of the pieces of furniture in his room.

When each child has placed his card correctly, ask him to give it back to you, saying where it was. If he has used an incorrect word or grammar, do not say that it is wrong but supply the correct sentence and have the child repeat it after you.

3 Following Instructions
These are first given by the teacher, but children must now do the actions by themselves.
Simon says:

       Close your eyes   Open your eyes

Pull your ears	Hold up two hands
Nod your head	Put both hands on table
Stand up	Stretch out your arms
Stand on one foot	Put both hands on head
Hold up one hand	Sit down.

4 Animal Noises

The teacher starts each sentence and the children supply the appropriate noise.

The bee says . . . ?
The cat says . . . ?
The cow says . . . ?
The dog says . . . ?
The donkey says . . . ?
The duck says . . . ?
The pig says . . . ?
The rooster says . . . ?
The sheep says . . . ?
The snake says . . . ?

5 Auditory Decoding and Appreciation of Rhyme

The teacher says the poem but the children respond with 'Yes' or 'No' to the various questions and also supply all the animal noises. The words to be supplied by the children are in italics.

What says a duck with a yellow back?
A yellow duck says '*quack quack quack*'.
Does a rooster sit on a fence and say 'moo'?
No, a rooster says '*cock a doodle doo*'.
And does a pig say '*oink oink oink*'?
Yes, a pig says '*oink oink oink*'.
What says a cow when she looks at you?
A brown-eyed cow says '*moo moo moo*'.
And does a dog say 'meow meow meow'?
No, a dog says '*bow wow wow*'.
And does a snake say '*sss sss sss*'?
Yes a snake says '*sss sss sss*'.
And does the sheep say 'he haw he haw'?
No, the sheep says '*baa baa baa*'.
The bee is helpful in what it does,
It kisses the flowers and says '*buzz buzz*'.

Now ask each child to state whether the following words rhyme or not.

back	quack
do	oink
does	buzz
meow	wow
moo	haw
you	sss

Now see if any of the children can think of other words to rhyme with back.

6   Story Time

The teacher tells the story of *Goldilocks and the Three Bears* this time (see p. 25), encouraging the children to supply what the bears said and did, making sure each child has an opportunity to respond. This is best done by looking at each child in turn when a response is required, and giving encouraging signals with eyes, hands and expression.

7   Singing and Rhythm

Singing nursery rhyme *Polly Put the Kettle On* (given to parents the previous week to practise at home). Use hand puppet to beat time to ensure children appreciate the rhythm and keep in time to the music. (A melodica or recorder is very useful here to supply a musical accompaniment.)

Polly put the kettle on,
Polly put the kettle on,
Polly put the kettle on,
We'll all have tea.
Suky take it off again,
Suky take it off again,
Suky take it off again,
They've all gone away.

8   Left, Right Discrimination

Stand up and recite the following action rhyme with left, right discrimination.

I am a teapot
Short and stout (*children bend knees and make circles at their sides to show how fat they are*)
Here's my handle (*put right hand on hip*)
And here's my spout (*put left arm up in a spout shape*)

Pick me up and pour me out (*children tilt to the left side where the spout is*).

Repeat several times.

9   Picture Description
Using large pictures with plenty of action in them, present one for each child and have him say what he thinks is happening. Discuss in some detail. A picture of a fairground is provided on the previous page, to be coloured in first.

10   Musical Bumps
Motor encoding. Children play on their own this time, without the teacher, to see if they can hear when the music stops without any assistance.

Finale
Line up for Smarties and positioning of the children as before. Each child shakes hands before he leaves and says Goodbye and Thank you.

Materials required
Two sheets of plain paper for each child, plus extra sheets for
 further drawing.
A pencil and rubber for each child.
Pictures of a doctor, soldier, fireman, milkman, dustman, postman,
 dentist and policeman.
Shape lotto.
Picture for discussion.

Concepts taught
Manual dexterity and social maturity—draw a man and draw a
 house test.
Rhythm patterning—clapping hands.
Acting—miming actions: washing, brushing hair, etc.
Vocabulary building and verbal reasoning.
Riddles—auditory decoding.
Vocal to motor—*Ten Little Men*
Left, right discrimination—*I am a teapot.*
Talk skills—picture for discussion: What's wrong?—the home.
The Farmer's in his Den—memory training.
Finale—social awareness.

1   Manual Dexterity and Social Maturity
Draw a man and draw a house test. Have ready two sheets of paper
for each child, clearly marked with his name, age, sex and date. Ask
the children to draw a man on one sheet and a house on the other
(see Appendix for norms). Further sheets of paper should be available for free drawing for those who have finished their assignment,
while waiting for everyone to finish the tests.
    Record the results, and make a note of which hand was used for
drawing.

2   Rhythm Patterning
All chant in unison, clapping hands to the following rhythm:

long	*long*	*short*	*short*	*short*
C l a p	c l a p	clap	your	hands

short	*short*	*short*	*short*	*l o n g*	*short*
Clap	your	hands	to-	g e t h	-er
l o n g	*l o n g*	*short*	*short*	*short*	
C l a p	c l a p	clap	your	hands	
short	*short*	*short*	*short*	*l o n g*	*short*
In	all	kinds	of	w e a t h	-er

3   Verbal-Motor Co-ordination

To the tune of 'Here we go round the Mulberry Bush' sing and mime the following actions:

This is the way we wash our face, wash our face, wash our face,
This is the way we wash our face on a cold and frosty morning.
This is the way we brush our hair, brush our hair, brush our hair,
This is the way we brush our hair, on a cold and frosty morning.
This is the way we clean our teeth, clean our teeth, clean our teeth,
This the way we clean our teeth, on a cold and frosty morning.
This is the way we tie our shoes, tie our shoes, tie our shoes,
This is the way we tie our shoes, on a cold and frosty morning.
This is the way we eat our cornflakes, eat our cornflakes, eat our
    cornflakes,
This is the way we eat our cornflakes, on a cold and frosty
    morning.
This is the way we drink our milk, drink our milk, drink our milk,
This is the way we drink our milk, on a cold and frosty morning.
This is the way we go to school, go to school, go to school,
This is the way we go to school, on a cold and frosty morning
    (*all marching around for this one*).

Make a note of which hand was used by each child for each of these activities.

4   Vocabulary Building and Verbal Reasoning

Show pictures of: doctor, soldier, fireman, milkman, dustman, postman, dentist, policeman. Ask each child in turn to name one. Then discuss what each of these people does and how it is helpful. For instance, ask the following questions:

In what ways are policemen helpful?
What would happen if you did not go to the dentist?
Why do you need to clean your teeth?
What would happen if there were no dustmen?
Are firemen very brave, or not?
Do soldiers need to be brave?
What do we mean by brave?

Would it matter if there were no milkmen to bring the milk to the
   door?
When do you need a doctor?
Does your illness or accident need to be serious or not?
If not, why not?

5 Riddles (auditory decoding)
The teacher starts each sentence and the children finish it.

He helps people get well—he is a . . . ?
He fights for his country—he is . . . ?
He puts out fires—he is a . . . ?
He collects the rubbish—he is a . . . ?
He looks after our teeth—he is a . . . ?
He brings the milk—he is a . . . ?
He brings the letters—he is a . . . ?
He shows us when to cross the street—he is a . . . ?

6 Visual Perception—Shape Lotto
Galt's picture lotto, where the children match different coloured
shapes shown on separate cards to the ones on their own cards.
Each child should have a different card, in that the shapes might be
the same but the colour will be different. For example, there may be
four circles of different colours and the child may only match the
circle that has the same colour as the one on his card.

These lotto games can equally well be made by the teacher as
shown below:

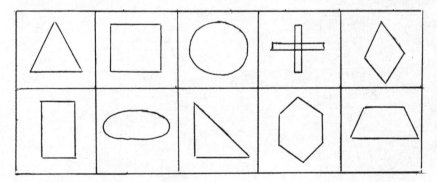

7 Ten Little Men—Manual Dexterity
Ten little men standing up straight
(*Hold up both hands with fingers straight*)

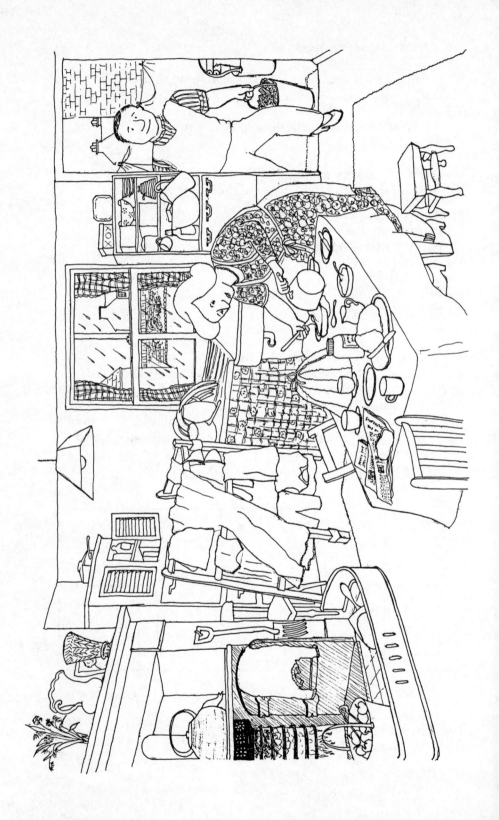

Ten little men open the gate
(*Open all fingers*)
Ten little men make a big ring
(*Join thumbs and little fingers to make a ring*)
Ten little men bow to the King
(*Bow hands down to table*)
Ten little men running to play
(*Run fingers all over table*)
Ten little men hiding away
(*Hide hands behind back*).

8   I Am a Teapot—Actions to Words and Left, Right Discrimination

I am a teapot short and stout (*children make a circle with their arms to show how fat they are*)
Here's my handle (*children put their right hands on hips for the spout*)
Here's my spout (*children put up their left arm in a spout shape*)
Pick me up and pour me out (*children lean to the left where the spout is to indicate pouring*).

9   Talk Skills—Picture for Discussion

A 'what's wrong?' picture of the home is provided opposite.
It should be coloured first. Ask the children to point out all the details that are wrong, and why.

10   The Farmer's in his Den

See p. 33 for words and accompanying actions.

Finale

Line up for Smarties, shake hands and say Goodbye and Thank you.

Materials required
Sheets of blank paper.
Six sheets with the following shapes drawn on them—circle, cross, square, triangle, diamond. This is for the Copying Shapes test.
Individual cards with six shapes drawn on them—seven sets of each, so that each child can be given a set and the teacher has a set. This is for visual sequencing of shapes. The cards should now have the following shapes on them: circle, square, triangle, diamond, oblong and hexagon.
Zoo animals.
Pictures of objects having a final 'p' or 'b' sound.
Tape recording of *Goldilocks and the Three Bears.*
Star chart and stick-on gold stars.
What's wrong? picture—the bedroom.

Concepts taught
Copying shapes on paper.
Visual sequencing—copying sequence with full range of shapes.
Visual perception—which shape is different?
Acting—miming further activities.
Listening and attention—*Goldilocks and the Three Bears* with children acting the parts.
Rhythm patterning—clapping hands *and* feet.
Visual perception—What's wrong in this picture? The bedroom.
Auditory memory—nursery rhymes and action rhymes without teacher leading the singing.
Closing activity—follow my leader.
Finale—social awareness.

1   **Opening Activity—Copying Shapes Test**
Have ready one sheet of paper for each child, clearly marked with his name, age and date, plus one set for each child of the following shapes for him to copy:

   circle, cross, square, triangle, diamond.

Allow spare paper for free drawing when task has been completed.
See p. 189 for norms and record achievement.

COPYING SHAPES TEST

Name   Age   Date

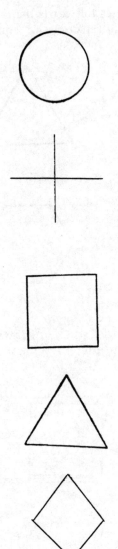

2   Visual Sequencing

With shapes as before, but using the full range of six shapes this time—circle, square, triangle, diamond, oblong and hexagon (see below). In other words, the teacher arranges her cards using four different shapes at any one time, and the children copy the sequence from their own set of shapes.

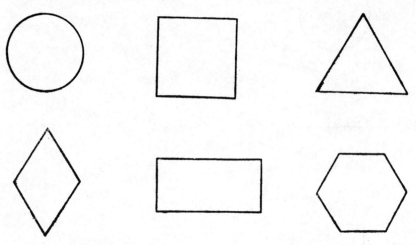

3   Visual Perception

'Which one is different?' with a series of shapes stuck or drawn on cards (see below). You can also use Philip and Tacy Geometry Rubber Stamps.

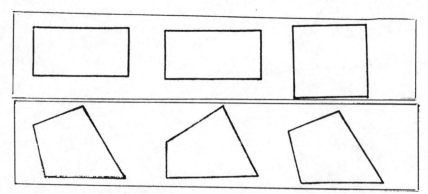

Each child is invited to say which shape is different from the others drawn on the card. Have a star chart so that success in recognising the shape that is different is given a star as reward (see last page of this session).

4   Miming (motor–vocal association)

Sing to the tune of *Here We Go Round the Mulberry Bush*.

This is the way we wash our clothes, wash our clothes, wash our
    clothes,
This is the way we wash our clothes, on a cold and frosty morning.
This is the way we iron our clothes, iron our clothes, iron our
    clothes,
This is the way we iron our clothes, on a cold and frosty morning.
This is the way we mow the lawn, mow the lawn, mow the lawn,
This is the way we mow the lawn, on a cold and frosty morning.
This is the way we paint the house, paint the house, paint the
    house,
This is the way we paint the house, on a cold and frosty morning.
This is the way we sweep the floor, sweep the floor, sweep the floor,
This is the way we sweep the floor, on a cold and frosty morning.
This is the way we wash the car, wash the car, wash the car,
This is the way we wash the car, on a cold and frosty morning.
(This one is best done standing round in a circle).

5   Listening and Attention

Play the story of *Goldilocks and the Three Bears* on the tape
recorder, with children and teacher joining in with words and
gestures. Each child can now be given a part to play and only speaks
when it is his turn to do so. They are now learning to 'take turns' in a
more meaningful way.

6   Vocabulary Building with Prepositions and Ear Training

Using zoo animals and pictures of objects having medial or final 'p'
or 'b'.
Prepositions: 'under', 'behind', 'between', 'beside', 'in front of'.
    Have the children choose a zoo animal which they place in front
of them. Discuss these animals, the countries they originally came
from and why some of them were hunted and shot. Hand out the
cards one at a time to each child, asking him to name it and then to
place it beside, in front of, under, behind or between one or more of
his animals. When all cards have been dealt, ask for them back: each
time the child must say where it was found.
    Then the zoo animals are replaced in their box, each child *naming*
the animal as he puts it away.

7   Rhythm Patterning

All chant in unison (teacher gradually drops out, leaving the
children to mark the beats, but she continues to say the words:

long	*long*	*short*	*short*	*short*	
Clap	clap	clap	your	hands	
short	*short*	*short*	*short*	*long*	*short*
Clap	your	hands	to-	geth	-er
long	*long*	*short*	*short*	*short*	
Clap	clap	clap	your	hands	
short	*short*	*short*	*short*	*long*	*short*
In	all	kinds	of	weath	-er
long	*long*	*short*	*short*	*short*	
Tap	tap	tap	your	toes	
short	*short*	*short*	*short*	*long*	*short*
Tap	your	toes	to-	geth	-er
long	*long*	*short*	*short*	*short*	
Tap	tap	tap	your	toes	
short	*short*	*short*	*short*	*long*	*short*
In	all	kinds	of	weath	-er

8   Visual Perception

What's wrong in the picture of the bedroom opposite? Each child is given the chance to spot something that is wrong and a count is made of the number of items correctly identified. Then the teacher discusses other things that are wrong and also why they are wrong. Colour the picture first.

9   Auditory Memory

Sing nursery rhyme *Polly Put the Kettle On*.

Polly put the kettle on,
Polly put the kettle on,
Polly put the kettle on,
We'll all have tea.
Suky take it off again,
Suky take it off again,
Suky take it off again,
They've all gone away.

Now sing *I am a tea pot*:

I am a tea pot
Short and stout (*children bend knees and make circles at their
    sides to show how fat they are*)
Here's my handle (*put right hand on hip*)
and here's my spout (*put left arm up in a spout shape*)
Pick me up and pour me out (*children tilt to the left side where the
    spout is*).

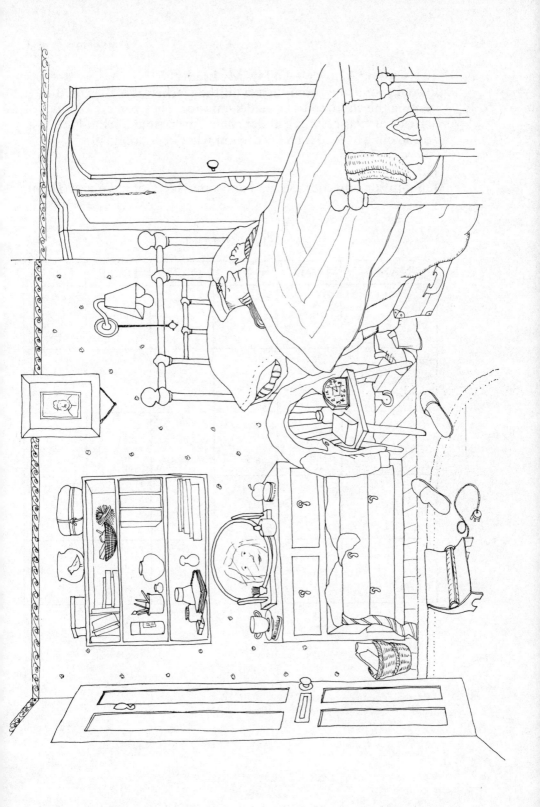

10   Closing Activity—Follow My Leader
Played round the room, first with the teacher as leader, and then
inviting the children to be leaders in turn. They can do all types of
activity such as crawling under chairs, over tables, behind the desk
and so on. The leader has to call out what he is doing.

Finale
Line up for Smarties. Shake hands and say Goodbye and Thank
you.

STAR CHART

NAME	DATE	DATE	DATE	DATE	DATE

Materials required
Sheets of paper with the following letters drawn on them:
  V T H O.
Plain sheets of paper.
Pencils with rubbers.
Further sheets with the following letters:
  X L A C U Y.
Music for *Polly Put the Kettle On* and *Oh Dear, What Can the Matter Be?*
Twelve small items on a tray, such as: safety pin, match, coin, pencil, rubber, pencil sharpener, scissors, comb, key, paper clip, spoon, cup.
Cards with pictures of different types of shops: butcher, baker, greengrocer, grocer, dairy, Post Office, clothing, furniture.
Lotto cards with pictures of objects with either medial or final 'p', 'b', 't', 'd', 'n', 'm', in them.

Concepts taught
Copying capital letters.
Rhyming and rhythm—*Polly Put the Kettle On* and *Oh Dear, What Can the Matter Be?*
Following instructions and attention.
Riddles to solve.
Action rhyme—*Ten Little Men.*
Classification—shops and the goods they stock.
Lotto—with medial and final 'p', 'b', 't', 'd', 'n', and 'm'.
Animal noises.
Physical control—statues.
Finale—social awareness.

1 **Opening Activity—Copying Letters** V T H O
Give each child a sheet of lined paper with the above letters written across the top. The letters should be the same height as the lines on the paper:

V T H O

If any of the children have difficulty in copying, write the letters faintly for the child to trace over them.

To reinforce the feel of the letters, have the children stretch out their arms so that the arms are straight and the index fingers touching. As they copy the teacher making the shapes, they should chant the names of the letters in unison. Repeat the movements, chanting the actions after naming the letters.

V—*Start at the top*—down to a point and up again.

T—*Start at the top*—down to the line—lift the pencil (indicate by bringing hands in to forehead and then out again)—cross the top from left to right.

H—*Start at the top*—down to the line—lift the pencil—start at the top again and down to the line—lift the pencil and draw a bar between the lines from left to right.

O—*Start at the top*—and make a circle meeting at the top again.

Now have the children draw these letters on their papers once more, continuing to chant the instructions. Note any improvement in performance. The teacher will have to demonstrate in mirror image, of course, as she will be standing facing the children. Some of the children may have no difficulty with this task and could be given the further list of letters to copy while the others continue practising the first set. These are the letters:

X L A C U Y

2 Rhyming and Rhythm—One
Singing:

Polly put the kettle on,
Polly put the kettle on,
Polly put the kettle on,
We'll all have tea.
Suky take it off again,
Suky take it off again,
Suky take it off again,
They've all gone away.

3 Rhyming and Rhythm—Two
Oh dear, what can the matter be?
Oh dear, what can the matter be?
Oh dear, what can the matter be?

Johnnie's so long at the fair.
He promised to buy me a piece of blue ribbon,
He promised to buy me a piece of blue ribbon,
He promised to buy me a piece of blue ribbon,
To tie up my bonny brown hair.

4   Motor Encoding and Verbal Comprehension
Simon Says
Now the complication is added where the actions are only obeyed if they have been preceded by 'Simon says'. Have several practice runs at first to ensure that *all* the children have understood.

Simon says	stand up
Simon says	run round chair once and sit down
	stamp your feet
Simon says	clap your hands
	bang the table
	nod your head
Simon says	pretend to cry
Simon says	pretend to sleep
Simon says	pretend to pour out tea

5   Riddles (auditory decoding)
I have wings, I fly in the air, what am I?
I have four wheels, you can ride in me, what am I?
I am round and yellow, I am very hot, what am I?
I come out at night and shine like diamonds in the sky, what am I?
I am soft and white and cold, and am only there in the winter,
    what am I?

6   Action Rhyme—Ten Little Men
Ten little men standing up straight
(Hold up both hands with fingers straight)
Ten little men open the gate
(Open all fingers)
Ten little men make a big ring
(Join thumbs and little fingers to make a ring)
Ten little men bow to the king
(Bow hands down to table)
Ten little men running to play
(Run fingers all over table)
Ten little men hiding away
(Hide hands behind back).

7   Classification

Using ESA shop cards, and pictures of things one would buy in them, ask each child to find all the things you would buy at the:

> fishmonger
> greengrocer
> butcher
> grocer
> baker
> dairy
> Post Office
> clothes shop

Each child should be given a shop, and when the picture of an object that would be in his shop is turned over, he calls out and names the object.

Explain that even in a supermarket the goods are still grouped into these categories, so it is no good going to the biscuit section to buy meat or fish.

8   Association

What noise do these animals make, and what do we get from them?
Cow, pig, duck, sheep, hen, bee.
(Each child to be given a turn to respond, with no prompting.)

9   Lotto

With medial or final 'p', 'b', 't', 'd', 'n', 'm', objects.
Play lotto, but ask the child who claims the card to say what sound he hears in the middle of the word or at the end of the word, as the case may be.

10   Closing Activity—Musical Statues

When the music stops, each child must remain perfectly still in whatever position he happens to be at the cessation of the music —like a statue in fact.

Finale

Line up for Smarties, shake hands, and say Goodbye and Thank you.

Materials required
Plasticine.
Cards depicting different rooms in a house (ESA Housecards).
LDA 'Wotami' tape.
Doll's house furniture.
Cards of objects with medial or final 'p', 'b', 't', 'd', 'm', 'n', sounds.
Picture of 'What's wrong?'—as in Session VI: the bedroom.

Concepts taught
Manual dexterity—plasticine and shape making.
Animal riddles—and appreciation of rhyme.
Listening and attention—*Goldilocks and the Three Bears*, with
    teacher only starting each sentence and children finishing it.
Prepositions—using all those that have appeared in earlier sessions.
Miming.
Finding 'what is wrong' in a picture—the bedroom.
Description of picture, saying what is happening.
The Farmer's in His Den.
Finale—social awareness.

1   **Opening Activity—Plasticine—Motor Dexterity**
Rolling the plasticine into long sausages, make the following shapes
with it:

V T H O X L A C U Y

2   **Riddles—Farm Animals Guessing Game**
The teacher says the rhyming poem. The children say what the
animal is after, 'What am I?'

> I give you milk,
> I say Moo,
> I have four legs,
> And give beef too.
> *What am I?*

I have four strong legs,
To carry you,
I eat green grass,
And yellow hay too.
What am I?

I lay eggs,
I give meat,
I hatch little chicks,
That say peep peep.
What am I?

I have four legs,
I catch the mice,
I'm furry and pretty,
You know I'm nice.
What am I?

Water quickly slides
Off my back,
I open my mouth
And say quack quack.
What am I?

3   Rhyming

The teacher now repeats the poem verse by verse, asking the children to say which words rhyme in each verse, or which words sound the same at the end. If this is not understood, go through each final word of each line saying, 'Milk, moo; do they sound the same?' 'Moo, legs; do they sound the same?' 'Moo, too; do they sound the same?' Repeat with each verse. The children can then listen to the LDA 'Wotami' tape and guess the animals.

4   Listening and Attention and Memory—Goldilocks and the Three Bears

The teacher reads *Goldilocks and the Three Bears* (see p. 25), but she only starts each sentence while the children supply the rest and provide the actions.

5   Classification—Vocal/Auditory Association

Using the ESA picture cards of rooms in a house, ask the children to name all the things one would find in:
    the living room
    the bedroom

the bathroom
the kitchen
the nursery

Each child is asked to say what he would expect to find in each of these rooms. If he can guess three things he is given the card and keeps it for the following activity. Other children may then be asked if they can think of anything else that could be found in these rooms.

6 Prepositions

—with doll's house furniture and 'p', 'b', 't', 'd', 'm', 'n', medial and final object cards.

The prepositions incorporate all those which have been used previously: 'in', 'on', 'under', 'beside', 'behind', 'between', 'over', 'under', 'through'. Each child is invited to select from the doll's house furniture those pieces which are appropriate for his room card (given in previous activity). The object cards are then handed to each child in turn; he names his card and is asked to place it in one of the positions given above, in relation to one of his pieces of furniture. When all cards have been correctly positioned, ask for them back, as before, and the child has to say where he found them.

7 What Am I Doing? (visual motor association)

Teacher acts out the following:

using telephone
driving car
reading book
threading needle
throwing ball
catching ball
writing
sewing
yawning

Then each child is invited to mime one of the activities while the other children and the teacher have to guess what he is doing. The children may also introduce a 'secret' activity of their own if they can think of one. Ask them to think of something for the next session.

8 What's Wrong?

Show the children a 'What's wrong?' picture—the bedroom from p. 51, or one of the ESA cards—and invite each one to find something 'wrong'. Have a 'star chart' prepared with the children's names on it. Each correct identification of something wrong earns a star. This is a good activity for promoting discussion as they can then all join in saying what is wrong and why.

9   Picture Description
Using the same 'What's wrong?' picture, have each child describe the picture to the others, while they or the teacher correct him. 'No, that is not what is happening, the man has not bothered to undress' (or whatever point the child is trying to make).

10   Closing Activity—The Farmer's in His Den
See p. 33 for words and accompanying actions.

Finale
Line up for Smarties, shake hands, and say Goodbye and Thank you.

Materials required
Puzzles, 4–5 year level.
Coloured bricks: cards with final 'k' and 'g' sounds.
Lotto with 'plurals'.
Picture cards representing different foods—bananas, chips, ham-
burgers, sausages, fish fingers, baked beans, fried eggs, bread,
butter, milk, Coca-Cola, apples, chocolates.
LDA 'Wotami' tape.
Star chart and self-adhesive stars.

Concepts taught
Visual perception, spatial awareness—puzzles.
Appreciation of colour—prepositions and final 'k', 'g'.
I spy—using colour.
Singing—all three nursery rhymes.
Talk skills—discussing what each child likes to eat.
Miming everyday action.
Lotto—with 'plurals'.
Follow my leader.
Finale—social awareness.

1   Opening Activity—Visual Motor Association
Puzzles of greater complexity—4–5 year level.

2   Prepositions
Using all the previously learned prepositions of position, cards of
objects ending in 'k' or 'g' and coloured bricks, proceed as follows:

Hand out to each child a given number of bricks of differing
colours. Have the child count the bricks and say what colours they
are.

Now ask each child which cards he would like from the pictures
of food. Play the 'prepositions game' by asking the child to put his
chosen food card in a given position in relation to a certain number
and colour of bricks. For example: put the bananas in between two
red-coloured bricks; put the apples behind four yellow bricks; put
the hamburger on three blue bricks—and so on until all cards have
been used and all children have had a turn.

Ask for the cards to be returned to you, saying where they were and the names of the foodstuffs as before.

3   Completing Phrases—Auditory Association

The teacher says the phrase, the children respond. The first one to do so on each phrase earns a star (see star chart, on last page of this session).

```
grass is . . . . . . . . . (green)
sky is . . . . . . . . . . . (blue)
bread and . . . . . . . (butter)
cup and . . . . . . . . . (saucer)
knife and . . . . . . (fork)
hat and . . . . . . . . (coat)
socks and . . . . . . (shoes)
```

4   'I Spy' Using Colour

The teacher starts this activity but then invites the children to spy something of a given colour—I spy something red, etc.

5   Singing Nursery Rhymes

Polly put the kettle on,
Polly put the kettle on,
Polly put the kettle on,
We'll all have tea.
Suky take it off again,
Suky take it off again,
Suky take it off again,
They've all gone away.

Oh dear, what can the matter be?
Oh dear, what can the matter be?
Oh dear, what can the matter be?
Johnnie's so long at the fair.
He promised to buy me a piece of blue ribbon,
He promised to buy me a piece of blue ribbon,
He promised to buy me a piece of blue ribbon,
To tie up my bonny brown hair.

Baa baa black sheep, have you any wool?
Yes sir, yes sir, three bags full,
One for the master, one for the dame,
And one for the little boy who lives down the lane.

6 Conversation

Using the food cards, ask the children in turn to say, and pick out the picture of, the foods they most enjoy eating. A discussion can then follow as to why they like or dislike certain foods and they may introduce other foods they enjoy. An insight can then be gained into the type of diet each child is receiving and the possibility of suggesting vitamin and mineral supplements.

7 Listening

Listening to further LDA 'Wotami' tapes and identifying the objects.

8 Miming—Visual and Auditory Association

Sing to the tune of *Here We Go Round the Mulberry Bush*:

This is the way we clap our hands, clap our hands, clap our hands,
This is the way we clap our hands, on a cold and frosty morning.
This is the way we stamp our feet, stamp our feet, stamp our feet.
This is the way we stamp our feet, on a cold and frosty morning.
This is the way we nod our head, nod our head, nod our head,
This is the way we nod our head, on a cold and frosty morning.
This is the way we stretch our arms, stretch our arms, stretch our arms,
This is the way we stretch our arms, on a cold and frosty morning.
This is the way we jump up and down, jump up and down, jump up and down,
This is the way we jump up and down, on a cold and frosty morning.

9 Lotto with 'Plurals'

The teacher turns over cards of single objects and the children have cards of several of the same objects. Each child has then to say, 'I have two (or three) hens, cats, boxes, cards, balls,' and so on.

10 Closing Activity

'Follow my Leader', round the room.

Finale

Line up for Smarties and shake hands, say Goodbye and Thank you.

STAR CHART

NAME	DATE	DATE	DATE	DATE	DATE

Materials required
Coloured shapes—LDA pattern blocks, or you may like to make
your own.
Jars or tins of different materials as before.
Bag of 2.5 cm (1 inch) red cubes.
Pictures of objects with initial, medial or final 'p', 'b', 't', 'd', 'm', 'n'.
Fruit and vegetable cards.
Pictures of reptiles, animals and insects for the children to colour.
Recorder.
Hand puppet.
Star char and gold stick-on stars.

Concepts taught
Shape sequencing.
Auditory discrimination—with musical notes.
Number work—with bricks, action and social vocabulary.
Singing all rhymes—one child conducting.
Prepositions and articulation work.
Riddles and talk skills.
Vocabulary building and colour.
Musical bumps.
Finale—social awareness.

1   **Opening Activity—Visual Perception, Sequencing
     and Memory**
Using the flat wooden shapes, the teacher makes a sequence of two
shapes. The children examine this for 20 seconds. Then the display
is covered and the children create the sequence from memory. If
they are successful with two shapes they can then proceed to
attempt three.

2   **Ear Training**
The teacher plays two notes on the recorder and the children state
whether it is the same note played twice or two different notes.
The same technique is used as with the tins containing different
materials, in that at first wide differences are presented, which
gradually become closer and closer until the sounds are only one
note apart.

3   Acting

The previous activities of pretending to be the postman, dustman, milkman, baker and so on, are now extended to include social interactions and number work. It will be necessary to represent the number of items by using the 2.5 cm cubes so that not only the giver of the items, but also the receiver can double-check that the right amount has changed hands.

Example

The milkman enters the group and says, 'Good morning, how many bottles of milk would you like today?' Each child in turn responds with:

'Good morning, I would like two bottles of milk, please.'

Two cubes then change hands. This dialogue is repeated by all the actors, who ask each child in turn how many items they wish to have; or how many the baker has brought, and so on. When the action is over, the children count to ten while the cakes are cooking in the oven, and then each child pretends to eat a cake, describing what kind of cake it is: chocolate, jam sponge, currant cake, cake with icing on, and so on.

4   Singing

Polly put the kettle on,
Polly put the kettle on,
Polly put the kettle on,
We'll all have tea.
Suky take it off again,
Suky take it off again,
Suky take it off again,
They've all gone away.

Oh dear, what can the matter be?
Oh dear, what can the matter be?
Oh dear, what can the matter be?
Johnnie's so long at the fair.
He promised to buy me a piece of blue ribbon,
He promised to buy me a piece of blue ribbon,
He promised to buy me a piece of blue ribbon,
To tie up my bonny brown hair.

Baa baa black sheep, have you any wool?
Yes sir, yes sir, three bags full,
One for the master, one for the dame,
And one for the little boy who lives down the lane.

One child puts on the hand puppet and becomes the conductor, beating time while the others sing.

5 Prepositions

—'in', 'on', 'under', 'behind', 'between', 'in front of', 'in the middle'.

Use bricks of the same colour so that only the concept of number is involved. Ask each child how many bricks he would like. He lines them up in front of himself and the teacher then hands out the cards with pictures of objects containing initial, medial or final 'p', 'b', 't', 'd', 'm', 'n', in them.

The *child* now decides where he is going to put his card and earns a star on the star chart for each card correctly placed (see last page of this session).

Another child then collects up the cards belonging to the child next door to him and says where he found each card and also the name of the child from whom he collected it. For example: 'I found the teddy in the middle of Johnnie's bricks.'

When all the cards have been collected in this way, each child puts his bricks back in the 'brick bag', counting them as he does so.

6 Riddles

The teacher says the riddle and the children guess the answer.

I hop across the field (rabbit)
I carry my house on my back (snail)
I leap in treetops (squirrel)
I slither through the grass (snake)
I jump into the pond (frog)
I swim in the lake (fish)
I have bright coloured wings (butterfly)
A cat likes to eat me (mouse)

7 Manual Dexterity—Colouring In

Have the children act out the animals and insects. Discuss the difference between animals, reptiles and insects. Have drawings of some of them for the children to 'colour in'.

8 Vocabulary Building with Colour Work

Using ESA fruit and vegetable cards, ask for volunteers to identify each by name. Repeat each response to give a good speech model. Have the group repeat in unison each response. Give each child a card to hold. Ask for the cards back by categories:

Give me all the red fruits
Give me all the green vegetables, etc.

9   Rhythm
Clapping—copying the teacher.

10   Closing Activity
Musical bumps.

Finale
Line up for Smarties, shake hands, and say Goodbye and Thank
you. Teachers should give parents copies of the stories and rhymes
that will be used in the next stage, so that the children may become
familiar with them by having them read to them before they start
Stage Two. If parents are working through the book at home, they
should read the stories and rhymes to their children before going on
to the next stage.

This is the last session until the next stage begins, so present each
child with a carnival novelty as a prize.

STAR CHART

NAME	DATE	DATE	DATE	DATE	DATE

STAGE TWO
SESSION I

Materials required
Star chart and stick-on gold stars.
Cards with a series of shapes on each card,
Four will be the same and one different.
Red crayons.
Plurals Lotto.
'Listening cards'—sound pictures.
'Looking cards'—hunt the 'k'.
Toy domestic animals.
Cards of words containing the 'k' sound in initial, medial or final
    positions.

Concepts taught
Copying letters.
Prepositions—'in', 'on', 'under', 'behind', 'in front of', 'between',
    'near', 'beside'.
Odd man out.
Story—*The Three Little Pigs.*
Lotto—plurals.
Listening and looking skills—finding the letter 'k'.
Articulation—tongue twisters.
Finger dexterity—*Five Little Soldiers.*
Memory and number work—*Peter Hammers with One Hammer.*
The Farmer's in his Den.
Finale—social awareness.

1   **Opening Activity—Visuo–motor Dexterity—Copying
    Letters—Writing Numbers**

V I H T O X A C A
(4 year level)

1 2 3 4 5 6 7 8 9 10
(5 year level)

2   Prepositions

—'in', 'on', 'under', 'behind', 'in front of', 'between', 'near', 'beside', 'underneath'.

Use with cards of objects containing the 'k' sound and the toy domestic animals. Let the children choose the animals they want to have and discuss why they have chosen those particular ones. Then deal the cards to each child. Have them name the objects, ensuring that they use correct pronunciation, and discuss the use of each object. Pictures could be something like the following:

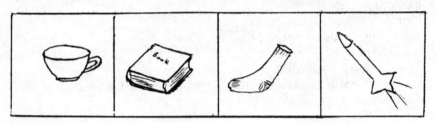

Ask the children in turn to place their cards in a stated position in relation to their animals. When all cards have been placed, ask each child to hand back his neighbour's cards, saying where he found them. For example, 'Tommy had the kettle underneath the pig.'

3   Picking the Odd One Out—Visual Decoding

Show the children cards with a series of shapes, only one of which differs from the rest on each card. (This is at a higher level than cards previously presented as the shapes are smaller and more diverse.)

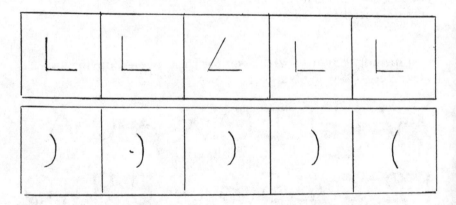

Invite each child in turn to state which one is different and why.

**4 Listening to Story Using Gesture—Auditory Decoding
and Motor Encoding**

Read the story *The Three Little Pigs*. Encourage the children to join
in and even take over from time to time, by asking what happens
next. Use gesture whenever appropriate.

THE THREE LITTLE PIGS

Once upon a time there was a mother pig who had three little pigs.
The three little pigs grew so big that their mother said to them,

'You are too big to live here any longer. You must go and build
houses for yourselves. But take care that the wolf does not catch
you.'

The three little pigs set off. Soon they met a man who was
carrying some straw. 'Please will you give me some straw?' asked
the first little pig. 'I want to build a house for myself.'

'Yes,' said the man, and he gave the little pig some straw. Then the
first little pig built himself a house of straw. He was very pleased
with his house. He said, 'Now the wolf won't catch me and eat me.'

'I shall build a stronger house than you,' said the second little pig.

Soon they met a man who was carrying some sticks.

'Please will you give me some sticks?' asked the second little pig. 'I
want to build a house for myself.'

'Yes,' said the man, and he gave the little pig some sticks. Then the
second little pig built himself a house of sticks. It was stronger than
the house of straw.

The second little pig was very pleased with his house. He said,
'Now the wolf won't catch me and eat me.'

'I shall build a stronger house than yours,' said the third little pig.

Soon he met a man who was carrying some bricks.

'Please will you give me some bricks?' asked the third little pig. 'I
want to build a house for myself.'

'Yes,' said the man, and he gave the third little pig some bricks.

Then the third little pig built himself a house of bricks. He was
very pleased with it. He said, 'Now the wolf won't catch me and eat
me.'

The next day the wolf came along. He came to the house of straw,
and knocked on the door and said, 'Little pig, little pig, let me come
in.'

'No, no,' said the little pig. 'By the hair of my chinny chin chin, I
will not let you come in.'

'Then I'll huff and I'll puff and I'll blow your house in,' said the
wolf.

So he huffed and he puffed, and the house of straw fell down and the wolf ate up the first little pig.

The next day the wolf walked further along the road. He came to the house of sticks, and he knocked on the door and said, 'Little pig, little pig, let me come in.'

'No, no,' said the little pig. 'By the hair of my chinny chin chin, I will not let you come in.'

'Then I'll huff and I'll puff and I'll blow your house in,' said the wolf.

So he huffed and he puffed, and the house of sticks fell down and the wolf ate up the second little pig.

The next day the wolf walked further along the road, and he came to the house of bricks, and knocked on the door.

'Little pig, little pig, let me come in,' said the wolf.

'No, no,' said the little pig. 'By the hair of my chinny chin chin, I will not let you come in.'

'Then I'll huff and I'll puff and I'll blow your house in,' said the wolf.

So he huffed and he puffed, but the house of bricks did not fall down.

When the wolf found he could not blow the house down he was very very angry indeed. He said, 'Little pig, I am going to eat you up. I am going to climb down your chimney to get you.'

The little pig was very frightened, but he said nothing. He put a big pot of water on the fire to boil.

The wolf climbed on to the roof, and then he began to come down the chimney. The little pig took off the lid from the pot. Into the pot fell the wolf, with a big splash. And that was the end of the wolf.

The third little pig was too clever for him.

5   **Lotto with Plural Cards**

A separate card must be available for every card on the lotto board.

Each child is given a board which must have different objects on it. The pack of cards of *two* of the same objects is then turned over one at a time and the child who has one of these objects on his lotto board calls out, 'I have two hands', and puts the card on his board where one hand is depicted. The first child to cover his board earns a star on the star chart (see last page of this session).

These star charts can be used until one child has filled a row, then another chart must be started. The charts should be kept and at the end of the year the number of stars can be added up and a small prize given to the child with the *most* stars.

Lotto cards—separate cards

Lotto board

6   Listening Skills

Children are each given a card with pictures of words, some with a 'k' sound in them and some without. They must listen for the 'k' and circle the picture with a red crayon when they hear the sound. If they hear the 'k' sound in 'box', that is excellent, as the letter 'x' sounds like 'ks'.

SOUND PICTURES

7   Looking Skills

Have cards with words on with the letter 'k' in them. The 'k' should be written on each card so the children know what they are looking for. They then circle the 'k' in red.

Hunt the 'k'

clock	kite	take	kite	skate
like	look	king	kill	sock
pick	bank	Jack	kettle	kiss
rank	make	naked	kind	unkind

As this is a *looking* task, the words must contain the letter 'k', whereas for *listening* we have had words which have both 'c' and 'k' to identify, as both letters had a 'k' sound in the pictures of *listening*.

8   Tongue Twister

She sells sea shells on the sea shore
The shells that she sells are not shells I am sure.

Now the teacher says the 'twister' very slowly and the children bang on the table when they hear 's' and put their fingers to their lips when they hear 'sh'.

9   Finger Play Rhymes

Peter hammers with one hammer, one hammer, one hammer
   (*hammer with one fist on the table*),
Peter hammers with one hammer all day long.
Peter hammers with two hammers, two hammers, two hammers
   (*hammer with two fists on the table*),
Peter hammers with two hammers all day long.
Peter hammers with three hammers, three hammers, three hammers
   (*hammer with two fists and one foot*),
Peter hammers with three hammers all day long.
Peter hammers with four hammers, four hammers, four hammers
   (*hammer with two fists and both feet*),
Peter hammers with four hammers all day long.
Peter hammers with five hammers, five hammers, five hammers
   (*hammer with two fists, both feet and nodding head*),
Peter hammers with five hammers all day long.
Peter's gone to sleep now, sleep now, sleep now,
Peter's gone to sleep now all day long
   (*put head on arms and pretend to be asleep*).

Five little soldiers

Standing in a row,

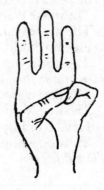

Three stood straight

And two stood so.

Along came the General

And what do you think?

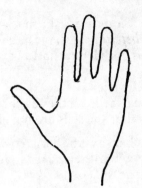

Up jumped those soldiers

As quick as a wink.

10   Closing Activity—The Farmer's in his Den
     The farmer's in his den,
     The farmer's in his den,
     Hey ho diddly oh,
     The farmer's in his den.
     The farmer wants a wife,
     The farmer wants a wife.
     Hey ho diddly oh,
     The farmer wants a wife.
(The child in the middle then chooses another child to be his wife.)
     The wife wants a child,
     The wife wants a child,
     Hey ho diddly oh,
     The wife wants a child.
(The 'wife' then chooses another child to be the 'child'.)
     The child wants a nurse,
     The child wants a nurse,
     Hey ho diddly oh,
     The child wants a nurse.
(The child then chooses a 'nurse'.)
     The nurse wants a dog,
     The nurse wants a dog,
     Hey ho diddly oh,
     The nurse wants a dog.
(The nurse then chooses a 'dog'.)
     The dog wants a bone,
     The dog wants a bone,
     Hey ho diddly oh,
     The dog wants a bone.
(The dog chooses a child to be the 'bone'.)

We all pat the dog,
We all pat the dog,
Hey ho diddly oh,
We all pat the dog.
(All the children pat the child who is the 'dog'.)

Finale
Line up for Smarties, shake hands, and say Goodbye and Thank
you.

STAR CHART

NAME	DATE	DATE	DATE	DATE	DATE

STAGE TWO
SESSION II

Materials required
Coloured threading beads and laces.
What's missing pictures.
Toy cowboys and Indians.
Shapes drawn on cards for children to colour in.
Cards of objects with 'g' or 'k' in them.
Number bingo cards and tiddlywinks.
Percussion instruments.

Concepts taught
Bead threading.
What's missing?
Singing—*Humpty Dumpty, Hickory Dickory Dock, Here We Go Round the Mulberry Bush.*
Rhythm—percussion instruments.
Story—*The Three Little Pigs.*
Number lotto.
Finger play rhymes—*Incy Wincy Spider, Here's the Lady's Knives and Forks, Peter Hammers with One Hammer.*
Prepositions.
Colouring in shapes.
Motor control and anticipation.
Finale—social awareness.

1   Sequencing, Colour and Memory Training

Give each child a box of coloured threading beads and a lace on to which to thread them.

The teacher threads the beads in a sequence and the children have to copy, making theirs exactly the same. Start with four beads, then build the sequence up to six.

Next have the children remember a sequence which the teacher lets them look at for five seconds and then covers. When the children have finished making theirs she uncovers her sequence and they check to see if they were right.

2   What's Missing in a Series of Pictures—Visual Perception

Draw about four pictures for each child to identify what's missing. The cards can then be shuffled up and dealt one at a time. The

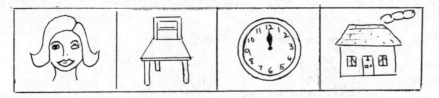

children have to shout out what is missing as the card is exposed, and the child who answers first earns a point.

3 Singing Nursery Rhymes—Memory and Rhyming

Humpty Dumpty sat on a wall,
Humpty Dumpty had a great fall,
All the King's horses and all the King's men,
Could not put Humpty together again.

Hickory, Dickory, Dock,
The mouse ran up the clock,
The clock struck one,
The mouse ran down,
Hickory, Dickory, Dock.

Here we go round the mulberry bush, the mulberry bush, the
    mulberry bush,
Here we go round the mulberry bush on a cold and frosty
    morning.
This is the way we clap our hands, clap our hands, clap our hands,
This is the way we clap our hands on a cold and frosty morning.
(Repeat with other actions.)

4 Rhythm

Now, singing the same rhymes, have the children beat the rhythm with a percussion instrument. If possible, have one child be the conductor to help the others keep time.

5 Listening

Story: *The Three Little Pigs* (see p. 71) with gestures, and the children supplying the recurring themes. For example, 'I'll huff and I'll puff and I'll blow your house down.'

6 Number Bingo with Numbers 1–20

Instructions must be given to the children, telling them that they only cover the number on their card with a counter if it has been called out. Do a trial run before playing.

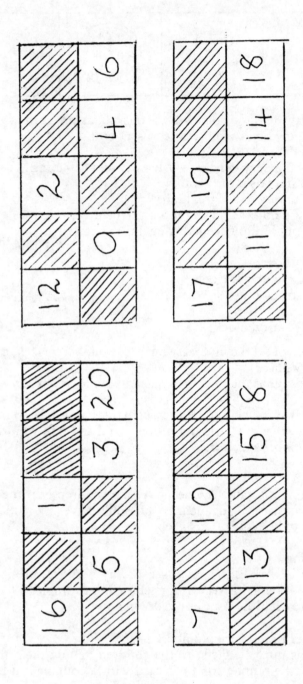

The children use the counters to cover the numbers when they are called out. The teacher must keep a record of the numbers she has called so that the child's card can be checked if he calls Bingo. He has to say what the numbers on his card are. The game can be played any number of times.

7   Finger Play Rhymes—Vocal–Motor Co-ordination
Incy wincy spider
Climbing up the spout,
Down came the rain
And washed the spider out,
Out came the sun
And dried up all the rain,
So incy wincy spider
Climbed up the spout again.

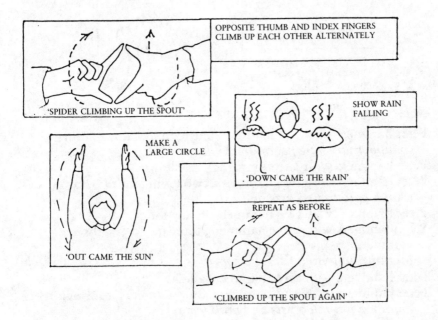

Here's the lady's knives and forks,
Here's the lady's table,
Here's the lady's looking glass,
And here's the baby's cradle.
Rock! Rock! Rock! Rock!

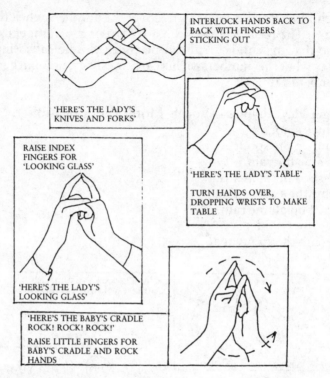

'HERE'S THE LADY'S KNIVES AND FORKS'

INTERLOCK HANDS BACK TO BACK WITH FINGERS STICKING OUT

RAISE INDEX FINGERS FOR 'LOOKING GLASS'

'HERE'S THE LADY'S TABLE'

TURN HANDS OVER, DROPPING WRISTS TO MAKE TABLE

'HERE'S THE LADY'S LOOKING GLASS'

'HERE'S THE BABY'S CRADLE ROCK! ROCK! ROCK!'

RAISE LITTLE FINGERS FOR BABY'S CRADLE AND ROCK HANDS

Peter hammers with one hammer, one hammer, one hammer
  (*hammer with one fist on the table*),
Peter hammers with one hammer all day long.
Peter hammers with two hammers, two hammers, two hammers
  (*hammer with two fists on the table*),
Peter hammers with two hammers all day long.
Peter hammers with three hammers, three hammers, three
  hammers
  (*hammer with two fists and one foot*),
Peter hammers with three hammers all day long.
Peter hammers with four hammers, four hammers, four hammers
  (*hammer with two fists and both feet*),
Peter hammers with four hammers all day long.
Peter hammers with five hammers, five hammers, five hammers
  (*hammer with two fists, both feet and nodding head*),
Peter hammers with five hammers all day long.
Peter's gone to sleep now, sleep now, sleep now,
Peter's gone to sleep now, all day long
  (*put head on arms and pretend to be asleep*).

8   Prepositions with Cowboys and Indians—Following Instructions

The children choose which they want to be—cowboys or Indians. They divide into teams.

Using the object cards with 'g' or 'k' in them, each team asks a member of the other team to place their card in any position they wish in relation to one of their cowboys or Indians, as the case may be.

The success of the team rests not only on the ability of the child to place his card correctly, but also on his ability to give the necessary instructions—in other words, giving and following instructions.

9   Manual Dexterity and Knowledge of Shapes

Have the children colour in the shapes drawn on the sheets of paper, making sure they do not go over the lines (see p. 84).

They then say what the names of the shapes are that they have coloured.

10   Closing Activity: Steps—Motor Control and Anticipation

The teacher is the leader in the first instance. She stands at one end of the room with her back to the children. The children stand at the other end.

The object is for the children to reach the teacher without being spotted moving. She turns round every so often to try to catch the children moving. The child who reaches her first becomes the leader, and so on.

Finale

Line up for Smarties, shake hands, and say Goodbye and Thank you.

SHAPES TO COLOUR

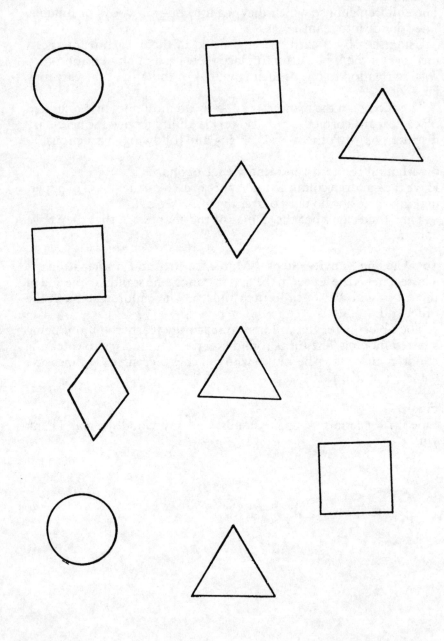

STAGE TWO
SESSION III

Materials required
Kaleidoscope.
Coloured threading beads and boxes to put them in.
Six small objects for Kim's game.
Small tray.
Drum.
Pictures with plenty of action in them.
Thimble.
Food cards.
Number bingo cards and tiddlywinks.

Concepts taught
Kaleidoscope—test for identifying favoured eye.
Classification.
Talk skills—food.
Rhythm—marching.
Finger play—*Incy Wincy Spider, Peter Hammers with One Hammer, Five Little Soldiers, Here's the Lady's Knives and Forks, Five Fat Gentlemen.*
Describing pictures.
What's missing?—Kim's game.
Memory training—*Goldilocks and the Three Bears.*
Number Lotto.
Hunt the Thimble.
Finale—social awareness.

1 Opening Activity—Eye Preference
Ask each child to look through the kaleidoscope and note which eye he is using.

2 Colour Work
Give each child a box of coloured beads and a threading lace.

Select one child to call out the colours as he threads the beads on his string. The others have to do as he says. Give each child an opportunity to be the leader unless he or she shows a marked disinclination to do so.

3   Classification—Auditory–Visual Association—Talk Skills

Using the food cards, ask the children to name the foods as the cards are presented to each child. When all the cards have been handed out, ask each child to say at what meal each of the foods on his card would be eaten—at breakfast, tea or dinner. The teacher then asks each child to give the cards back according to colour: for example, 'Give me all the red foods', etc.

Talk about the children's favourite foods and rate them one to nine in order of preference. Make a note for future reference. Make sure each child expresses himself in full sentences. The teacher should repeat the child's utterance to give a good speech model, especially if the child's pronunciation or grammar is not as good as it should be—for example:

Child: 'I like bananas much more better than apples.'

Teacher: 'I see, Tommy, you like bananas better than apples —what about you Jane?' and so on.

4   Rhythm

The teacher beats a drum in a marching rhythm while the children march round the room following the rhythm, which will vary in tempo and volume.

If there is a piano and the teacher can play it, so much the better. A child could then take over the beating of the drum and the others follow the rhythm. Each child can have a turn at beating the drum.

5   Finger Play Rhymes—Auditory–Motor Association

Incy wincy spider
Climbing up the spout,
Down came the rain
And washed the spider out,
Out came the sun
And dried up all the rain,
So incy wincy spider
Climbed up the spout again.

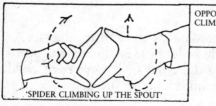

OPPOSITE THUMB AND INDEX FINGERS
CLIMB UP EACH OTHER ALTERNATELY

'SPIDER CLIMBING UP THE SPOUT'

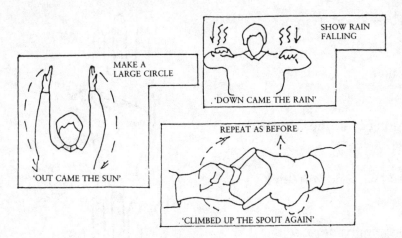

Peter hammers with one hammer, one hammer, one hammer
  (*hammer with one fist on the table*),
Peter hammers with one hammer all day long.
Peter hammers with two hammers, two hammers, two hammers
  (*hammer with two fists on the table*),
Peter hammers with two hammers all day long.
Peter hammers with three hammers, three hammers, three
  hammers (*hammer with two fists and one foot*),
Peter hammers with three hammers all day long.
Peter hammers with four hammers, four hammers, four hammers
  (*hammer with two fists and both feet*),
Peter hammers with four hammers all day long.
Peter hammers with five hammers, five hammers, five hammers
  (*hammer with two fists, both feet and nodding head*),
Peter hammers with five hammers all day long.
Peter's gone to sleep now, sleep now, sleep now,
Peter's gone to sleep now, all day long
  (*put head on arms and pretend to be asleep*).

Five little soldiers
Standing in a row

Three stood straight

And three stood so.

Along came the General

And what do you think,

Up jumped those soldiers

As quick as a wink.

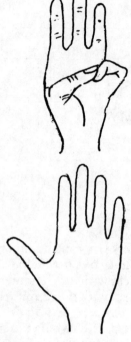

Here's the lady's knives and forks,
Here's the lady's table,
Here's the lady's looking glass,
And here's the baby's cradle.
Rock! Rock! Rock! Rock!

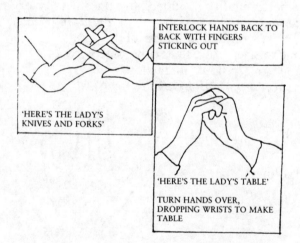

INTERLOCK HANDS BACK TO
BACK WITH FINGERS
STICKING OUT

'HERE'S THE LADY'S
KNIVES AND FORKS'

'HERE'S THE LADY'S TABLE'

TURN HANDS OVER,
DROPPING WRISTS TO MAKE
TABLE

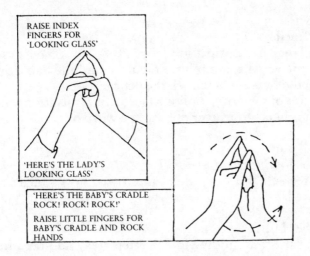

Five fat gentlemen standing in a row (*hold up five fingers*),
Five fat gentlemen bow down low (*bow heads to table*),
Five fat gentlemen walk across the floor (*walk with fingers across the table*),
Don't forget, gentlemen, please close the door (*clap hands*).

6   Picture Description—Visual Perception and Expressive Ability

Using the action picture, have the children describe what they think is going on. They will probably need some prompting to elicit the full expressive ability of each child.

7   Kim's Game—Visual Memory and Perception

The teacher arranges the six small objects on the tray and displays it to the children for ten seconds. She tells them to try to remember all the things on the tray as one will be removed each time the tray is covered. After ten seconds the teacher covers the tray and slips one of the objects into her pocket. The tray is then exposed and the children guess what has gone until all of them have been removed.

The objects are then replaced, the children look at them again, then they are covered and the children try to remember what the objects were. They could then be given their first lesson in memorising lists of things by association.

Each item is listed:

1   Comb
2   Button
3   Hair grip
4   Key

     5   Scissors
     6   Pencil

Each child then makes up a silly story using each object in sequence —for example, 'The comb hit the button and the hair grip turned the key in the scissors to unlock the pencil.'

The secret of memorisation is to form an association with something that is likely to trigger the wanted word or name.

8   Story Time

Return to *Goldilocks and the Three Bears* (see p. 25), but have the children tell the story this time to see how much they have remembered.

9   Number Lotto

Using the cards and tiddlywink counters, play number bingo as in Session II.

10   Closing Activity—Hunt the Thimble

One child leaves the room while the others sit around on the floor in a circle. The thimble is secreted under one of them. The child outside then returns and is directed to the thimble by the other children shouting 'hot' or 'cold', according to whether the seeker is approaching or receding from the place of concealment.

Finale

Line up for Smarties, shake hands, and say Goodbye and Thank you.

Materials required
Wooden puzzles of 20 or 30 pieces each.
People cards.
Zoo animals.
Plurals lotto.
Ten small objects and a small tray.
Number lotto.
Two sets of wooden or plastic numbers.
Cards with objects beginning with 'j' or 'ch'.

Concepts taught
Jigsaw puzzles.
People cards.
Prepositions—with zoo animals.
Story—*The Three Little Pigs*.
Irregular plurals lotto.
Singing—with rhythm songs.
Kim's game.
'Simons Says'—parts of the body.
Following instructions.
Number relay race.
Finale—social awareness.

1 Opening Activity—Visuo-Spatial Perception

Jigsaw puzzles of more complex forms—20 to 30 piece jigsaw puzzles. The children will need guidance on first selecting the pieces with the straight edges to go round the outside and matching up the colours—blues for the sky, greens or browns for the ground, and so on.

The children exchange puzzles when they have finished their own.

2 People Cards—Visual and Auditory Decoding

Use the people cards (ESA Street Pictures—People who work for us) or ones drawn by the teacher: newspaper man, road sweeper, window cleaner, road mender, coalman, milkman, policeman, ice cream man, flower woman, postman, dustman.

The child first identifies each picture by naming it. If in difficulty the teacher supplies the names and the cards are laid out on the table.

Each child then picks out the appropriate card in response to riddle-type questions such as:

'Who brings the letters in the morning?'

'Who clears away the rubbish?'

and so on.

3   Prepositions and Zoo Animal Families

Using all the prepositions of place previously learnt in conjunction with zoo animal families.

First invite each child to select a family—lion, lioness, cubs; stag, hind, calf; explain that this one is the father, this one the mother and these are the children.

When each child has a family of animals, discuss the difference between wild animals, zoo animals and domestic animals.

Now take the cards of objects or verbs beginning with the sound 'j' or 'ch', and give one to each child. Ask him to name it and then to place it in a position of his own choosing among his animal family, saying where he is putting it.

Now gather up the cards and play a game of snap, where the children call 'snap' when two cards are showing which both have the sound 'j' at the beginning, or both have the sound 'ch' at the beginning.

4   Listening and Motor Decoding

Read *The Three Little Pigs* (see p. 71), inviting the children to take over the story wherever they are able.

5   Plurals Lotto—with Irregular Plurals

mouse—mice	man—men
house—houses	leaf—leaves
sheep—sheep	loaf—loaves
goose—geese	tooth—teeth
woman—women	foot—feet

Each child has a card with pictures of two of the above objects on. The teacher turns over the individual cards depicting one of the objects. The child who has two of that object says, 'I have two mice,' or 'I have two loaves,' etc.

The child whose card is full first is the winner.

6   Singing and Rhythm

Singing all the nursery rhymes. The children should sing and also beat out the rhythm with their hands on the table.

Humpty Dumpty sat on a wall,
Humpty Dumpty had a great fall,
All the King's horses and all the King's men
Could not put Humpty together again.

Jack and Jill went up the hill
To fetch a pail of water,
Jack fell down and broke his crown
And Jill came tumbling after.

Hickory, dickory, dock,
The mouse ran up the clock,
The clock struck one,
The mouse ran down,
Hickory, dickory, dock.

Ding dong dell, pussy's in the well,
Who put her in?
Little Tommy Thin.
Who pulled her out?
Little Tommy Stout.
What a naughty boy was that
To try to drown poor pussy cat
Who n'ere did any harm
But killed all the mice in farmer's barn.

7   What's Missing? Visual Perception

Using the 'what's missing' pictures from LDA, or drawn by the teacher, each child states what is missing and what sort of things the people or object will be unable to do because of these missing parts.

8   Following Instructions—Knowledge of Parts of the Body—Left–Right Discrimination

Simon says:

Raise your right arm
Put it down
Touch the top of your head
Touch your chin
Touch your left ear
Turn round to the right
Sit down
Stand up

Touch your toes
Touch your ankle
Touch your knee
Touch your thigh
Touch your waist
Yawn
Laugh
Sit down.

9   Number Lotto

Matching the symbols which are depicted on the individual cards presented by the teacher to the number of objects the child has on his picture lotto card.

Teacher's Cards

Children's Lotto Boards

10   Closing Activity—Number Relay Race

Place the sets of wooden or plastic numbers randomly on separate tables at the end of the room. Divide the children into teams. On the word 'go' the first child runs to the table and picks up the number 1 and runs back to give it to the next child. He puts it on the table behind him and runs to pick up number 2, returning to hand it to the next child who places it in sequence beside number 1, then runs to pick up number 3, and so on.

Finale

Line up for Smarties, shake hands, and say Goodbye and Thank you.

Materials required
Plasticine.
ESA cards of household objects.
Tiny pieces of sticky paper, such as the edging to stamps.
Tracking square for the letter 'b'.
Star chart and stick-on gold stars.

Concepts taught
Plasticine modelling.
Cards of household objects.
'Simon says'—parts of the body.
Riddle rhyme—*Two Little Dickie Birds*.
Finger play rhymes—*Five Fat Gentlemen, Five Little Soldiers*.
Story—*Snow White and the Seven Dwarfs*.
Acting—Postman, milkman, etc.
Tracking letter 'b'.
Odd man out.
The Farmer's in his Den.
Finale—social awareness.

1   Opening Activity—Manual Dexterity and Number Work

Using plasticine, give each child several small lumps of the same colour so that the colours do not become mixed at the end of the activity. Have the children roll their small lumps into long, thin strips. They then shape them into numbers. You may need a number card for the children to copy.

When they have successfully made their numbers, have them roll them back into one big ball (of the same colour) and return it to the plasticine box.

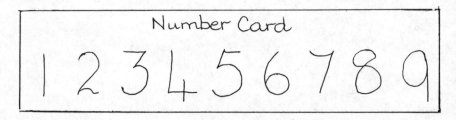

2 Using the ESA Household Object Cards

Deal the cards out to the children and then have them lay each card on the table one at a time, naming the object and saying what it is used for. Some discussion could then follow about other uses the objects could be put to, to encourage lateral thinking. For example:

Doorstop: To keep the door open
To hit a burglar on the head
To drop on grandma's toe
To stop papers blowing about
To make the cat sit still by putting it on her tail
For daddy to trip over when he comes home.

3 Following Instructions and Knowledge of Left or Right

Simon says:

Go to the left-hand window
Turn to the right
Take five paces forward
Turn to the left
Run to the right side of the door
Hop on right foot back to the window
Turn to the left
Skip right round the room and back to your own chair.

4 Two Little Dickie Birds Riddle

Do not disclose the secret of this finger rhyme but keep the children guessing how it is done.

Two little dickie birds
Sitting on a wall,
One named Peter,
One named Paul.
Fly away, Peter,
Fly away, Paul,
Come back, Peter,
Come back, Paul.

A piece of sticky paper is applied to the first finger of each hand; on the line, 'fly away, Peter', etc., each hand in turn is put behind the head, and when it is brought back again the middle finger is displayed showing no sticky paper. When the birds are exhorted to come back the same procedure takes place but the first fingers are now displayed, showing the sticky paper once more.

5   Finger Play Rhymes
Five fat gentlemen standing in a row (*hold up five fingers*),
Five fat gentlemen bow down low (*bow heads to table*),
Five fat gentlemen walk across the floor (*walk with fingers across
   the table*),
Don't forget, gentlemen, please close the door (*clap hands*).

Five little soldiers
Standing in a row (*hold up five fingers*),
Three stood straight
And three stood so (*keeping three fingers straight, bend little finger
   and thumb across palm*).
Along came the General
And what do you think?
Up jumped those soldiers
As quick as a wink (*hold up all five fingers again*).

6   Listening and Memory
Read the story of *Snow White and the Seven Dwarfs* and ask the
children about it afterwards—particularly the names of the Seven
Dwarfs.

SNOW WHITE AND THE SEVEN DWARFS

Once upon a time a beautiful young Queen was sewing by the
window. It was snowing outside, and when the Queen accidentally
pricked her finger a few drops of blood fell on the snow. She thought
how beautiful it looked against the white. Soon afterwards, she had
a baby girl and called her Snow White. However, the poor Queen
died when the baby was born and Snow White's father married
again. Although very beautiful, the new Queen was a proud and
vain woman. Every day she looked in her magic mirror and asked:

> 'Mirror, mirror on the wall,
> Who is fairest of them all?'

Each day the mirror replied: 'You, Queen, are the fairest one of all.'
   When Snow White grew up she was very beautiful, with a white
skin, rosy red cheeks and long black hair. One day, when the Queen
looked in the mirror and asked who was the fairest of them all, the
mirror replied:

> 'O Queen! Thou art fair as fair can be,
> But Snow White is more fair than thee.'

When the Queen heard this, she became very jealous.

As the days passed and the mirror always said Snow White was the fairest of them all, the wicked Queen could bear it no longer and told the royal huntsman to take Snow White into the forest and kill her and bring back her heart. However, the huntsman was a kind man and could not kill Snow White. He let her go in the forest and killed a deer so that he could take its heart back to the wicked Queen. She was quite satisfied and thought Snow White was dead.

When it became dark in the forest, Snow White was frightened and ran and ran until she came to a little cottage. She knocked, but no one was in, so she looked inside. Seven places were laid on the table and upstairs were seven small beds. She was tired and fell asleep on one of them. After a while the seven dwarfs, who were called Doc, Happy, Grumpy, Sleepy, Sneezy, Dopey and Bashful, came home and found her asleep, but they did not wake her. In the morning she told them her story and they said she could stay if she cooked and cleaned for them, so she did.

One day the wicked Queen decided to ask her mirror who was the fairest of them all. As always, she said:

> 'Mirror, mirror, on the wall,
> Who is fairest of them all?'

And the mirror replied:

> 'You, Queen, both fair and lovely are,
> But over the hills, in the Greenwood dell,
> Where the seven dwarfs do work and dwell,
> Snow White is safely hidden, and she
> Is fairer far, O Queen, to see.'

The Queen was very angry when she realised that Snow White was alive after all, and decided to kill her herself.

She dressed up like an old pedlar and went to the cottage. She took with her some red apples, one of which was poisoned. She persuaded Snow White to eat the poisoned apple and when she bit it she fell down dead. The wicked Queen cackled with delight because now she knew she would be the fairest one of all.

She rushed home and looked in the mirror.

> 'Mirror, mirror on the wall,
> Who is the fairest one of all?'

And the mirror replied: 'You, Queen, are the fairest one of all.'

Then at last her jealous heart was satisfied that her beautiful step-daughter was well and truly dead.

The dwarfs tried all they could to revive her but it was no use, so they put her in a glass coffin so that everyone could see her and each dwarf in turn watched over her. Her beauty did not fade and she seemed to be sleeping.

One day a prince came riding in the forest and saw Snow White in her glass coffin. He fell in love with her and decided to take her in her coffin back to his kingdom. On the way, one of his servants tripped over a root and dropped the coffin. The jolt made the poisoned piece of apple fall out of Snow White's mouth and immediately she began to come back to life.

When the prince realised she was alive, he asked her to marry him. So they were married in his kingdom with much rejoicing and lived happily ever after.

The poor Queen, though, was so upset when her mirror told her that Snow White had come back to life that she fell down dead.

7   Acting—Expressive Motor Skills and Motor Decoding
Act the parts of all the street people who were talked about in Session IV, when we used ESA street pictures.

Each child who guesses the person acted by another child earns a star on the star chart (see last page of this session).

8   Tracking Sheets
Use one sheet for each child (see opposite), and have them track from left to right, crossing off the letter 'b' each time they come to it.

A model of the letter 'b' should be on a card in front of them.

9   Listening Skills
Which of these words do *not* begin with 'j'?

    Jam, ham, chum, jug, jump.
    Joy, Jill, chill, Joan, chip.

The words should be said slowly in groups of five. The children bang the table when they hear a word which DOES NOT begin with the sound 'j'.

10   Closing Activity
The Farmer's in his Den (see p. 33 for the full song).

Finale
Line up for Smarties, shake hands, and say Goodbye and Thank you.

'b'
TRACKING

c	h	i	b	d
z	e	b	j	k
b	l	m	d	n
y	b	x	b	a
f	g	b	q	b

STAR CHART

NAME	DATE	DATE	DATE	DATE	DATE

STAGE TWO
SESSION VI

Materials required
Prepared drawings for colouring in, traced from a colouring book of *Winnie the Pooh* or other suitable simple line drawings of known characters.
ESA clothing cards.
Number dominoes—LDA or made by the teacher.
Picture for talking skills.
Shape dominoes.

Concepts taught
Colouring—prepared drawings (*Winnie the Pooh*).
Finger play—*Church and Steeple, Five Fat Gentlemen*.
Clothing cards and classification.
Matching numerals to objects—number dominoes.
Talking skills—picture description.
Number rhyme.
Matching shapes and sizes.
Tense.
Singing—*Here We Go Round the Mulberry Bush*.
Looby Loo.
Finale—social awareness.

1   Opening Activity
Colouring prepared drawings traced from a copy of *Alice's Adventures in Wonderland* (see overleaf).

2   Finger Play
Here's the church
And here's the steeple,
Open the doors
And see all the people.
Here is the parson
Going up stairs,
And here he is in the pulpit
Saying his prayers.

INTERLOCK FINGERS FOR ROOF OF CHURCH

'HERE IS THE CHURCH'

RAISE INDEX FINGERS FOR STEEPLE

'AND HERE'S THE STEEPLE'

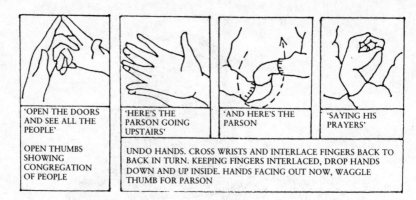

'OPEN THE DOORS AND SEE ALL THE PEOPLE'

OPEN THUMBS SHOWING CONGREGATION OF PEOPLE

'HERE'S THE PARSON GOING UPSTAIRS'

'AND HERE'S THE PARSON

'SAYING HIS PRAYERS'

UNDO HANDS. CROSS WRISTS AND INTERLACE FINGERS BACK TO BACK IN TURN. KEEPING FINGERS INTERLACED, DROP HANDS DOWN AND UP INSIDE. HANDS FACING OUT NOW, WAGGLE THUMB FOR PARSON

Five fat gentlemen standing in a row (*hold up five fingers*),
Five fat gentlemen bow down low (*bow heads to table*),
Five fat gentlemen walk across the floor (*walk with fingers across
     the table*),
Don't forget, gentlemen, please close the door (*clap hands*).

3   Clothing Cards
Identifying them then picking out which ones would be suitable for
a girl and which for a boy. Then—the things you wear on your feet,
the things you would wear when it is hot, rainy or cold. The clothes
that pull over your head, and the clothes that have buttons.

4   Lotto (Galt—or Prepared by the Teacher)
Number dominoes—matching objects to symbols (see opposite).

5   Picture Description
Using an action picture, have the children describe it and discuss it.

6   Number Rhyme
One, two, buckle my shoe,
     (*pretend to do up shoe*)
Three, four, knock on the door,
     (*make two knocks on the table*)
Five, six, pick up sticks,
     (*pretend to pick up sticks*)
Seven, eight, lay them straight,
     (*pretend to lay them straight*)
Nine, ten, a big fat hen.
     (*make a big circle with arms to show the fat hen*)

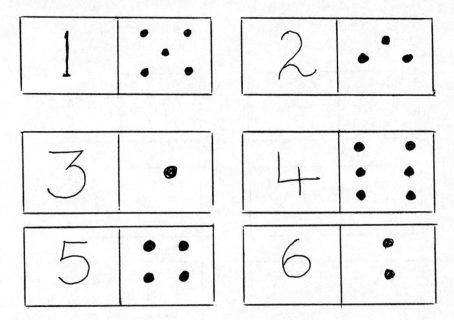

7 Shape Dominoes and Discrimination of Size
Obtain from LDA or can be made by the teacher (see p. 108). Only the shape of the same size can be matched.

8 Appreciation of Tense
Say to each child in turn: 'If I *do* something today, tomorrow I will have *done* it.' Explain that *do* is what you are *doing* now but *done* is what you have already *done*. It is in the past—it has already happened.

Continue until the children understand the concept of present and past tense. Then try to elicit the correct responses by saying:

'I *jump* over the fence today but John . . . . . . over it yesterday.'

'I *am walking* to the door now, but last week I . . . . . . to the shops.'

'It *is* now four o'clock, but it . . . two o'clock two hours ago.'

'I *am having* my birthday today. John . . . his two weeks ago.'

'I *have* three kittens. Two years ago I . . . four kittens but one died.'

9 Nursery Rhyme
Here we go round the mulberry bush, the mulberry bush, the mulberry bush,

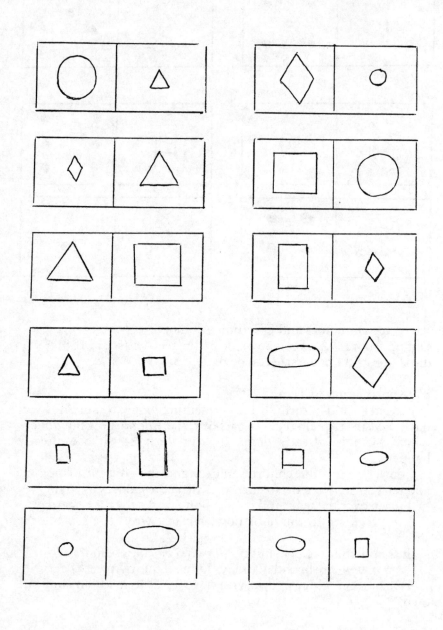

Here we go round the mulberry bush on a cold and frosty morning.
This is the way we clap our hands, clap our hands, clap our hands,
This is the way we clap our hands on a cold and frosty morning.
(Repeat with other actions.)

10 Closing Activity—Left–Right Discrimination
Here we go looby loo,
Here we go looby light,
Here we go looby loo,
All on a Saturday night.

a)   You put your right hand in,
     You put your right hand out,
     You put your right hand in,
     And shake it all about,
     You do the hokey cokey and turn around,
     And that's what it's all about.

b)   *Continue with left hand, right and left foot.*

Finale
Line up for Smarties, shake hands, and say Goodbye and Thank
you.

Materials required
Peg mosaics.
Coloured blocks—2.5 cms (one inch).
Number cards with numerals 1 to 9.
Matching shape cards.

Concepts taught
Manual dexterity and awareness of space—mosaics and pattern making.
Colour work—using coloured blocks.
Number work—*One, Two, Buckle My Shoe*, 'Simon Says'.
Matching shapes—visual perception.
Finger play—*Five Fat Gentlemen, Church and Steeple, Here's the Lady's Knives and Forks*.
Patterning—copying a clapped pattern.
Story—*Snow White and the Seven Dwarfs*.
Nursery songs.
Nursery rhymes—fine motor dexterity.
Ring a Ring of Roses.
Finale—social awareness.

1 Opening Activity—Manual Dexterity, Awareness of Space
Peg mosaics and pattern making.

2 Colour work
Food cards are identified and laid on the table. Hand out coloured blocks to each child. Let him choose a food the same colour as his block. Call on each child to hold up his block and tell the class in a complete sentence what the food is and what colour it is. For example: 'This is a salad, it is green.'

3 Number Work
One, two, buckle my shoe,
(pretend to do up shoe)
Three, four, knock at the door,
(make two knocks on the table)

Five, six, pick up sticks,
  (pretend to pick up sticks)
Seven, eight, lay them straight,
  (pretend to lay them straight)
Nine, ten, a big fat hen.
  (make a big circle with arms to show the fat hen)

Then do the rhyme again, holding up appropriate number cards which have been dealt to the children.

Simon says—holding up different numbers of fingers.

4   Matching Shapes—Visual Perception

Use small cards each with a single shape on it, to be matched with a large card showing six different shapes to choose from. The children are dealt cards with all these shapes on them, and see how quickly they can match them to the shapes on the large card. Shapes: hexagon, elipse, kite, trapezium, octagon, right-angled triangle.

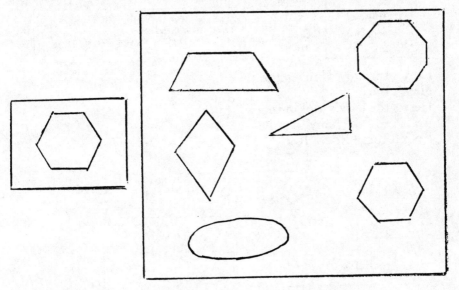

5   Finger Play

Five fat gentlemen standing in a row (*hold up five fingers*),
Five fat gentlemen bow down low (*bow heads to table*),
Five fat gentlemen walk across the floor (*walk with fingers across table*),
Don't forget, gentlemen, please close the door (*clap hands*).

Here's the church
And here's the steeple,
Open the doors
And see all the people.
Here is the parson
Going up stairs,
And here he is in the pulpit
Saying his prayers.

INTERLOCK FINGERS FOR ROOF OF CHURCH

'HERE IS THE CHURCH'

RAISE INDEX FINGERS FOR STEEPLE

'AND HERE'S THE STEEPLE'

'OPEN THE DOORS AND SEE ALL THE PEOPLE'

OPEN THUMBS SHOWING CONGREGATION OF PEOPLE

'HERE'S THE PARSON GOING UPSTAIRS'

'AND HERE'S THE PARSON

'SAYING HIS PRAYERS'

UNDO HANDS. CROSS WRISTS AND INTERLACE FINGERS BACK TO BACK IN TURN. KEEPING FINGERS INTERLACED, DROP HANDS DOWN AND UP INSIDE. HANDS FACING OUT NOW, WAGGLE THUMB FOR PARSON

Here's the lady's knives and forks
Here's the lady's table,
Here's the lady's looking glass
And here's the baby's cradle.
Rock! Rock! Rock! Rock!

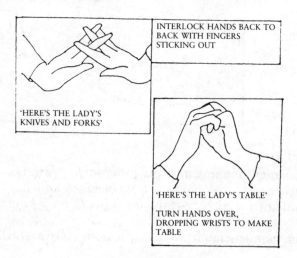

INTERLOCK HANDS BACK TO BACK WITH FINGERS STICKING OUT

'HERE'S THE LADY'S KNIVES AND FORKS'

'HERE'S THE LADY'S TABLE'

TURN HANDS OVER, DROPPING WRISTS TO MAKE TABLE

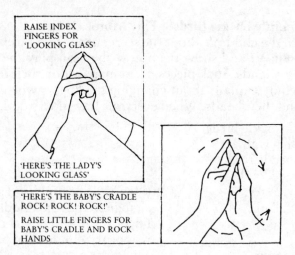

RAISE INDEX
FINGERS FOR
'LOOKING GLASS'

'HERE'S THE LADY'S
LOOKING GLASS'

'HERE'S THE BABY'S CRADLE
ROCK! ROCK! ROCK!'

RAISE LITTLE FINGERS FOR
BABY'S CRADLE AND ROCK
HANDS

6 Patterning

Listen and count how many times I clap—then try to copy. Teacher claps a given number. Afterwards she claps a rhythm of loud and soft for the children to copy.

7 Listening to a Story and Actions—Auditory to Motor

Read *Snow White and the Seven Dwarfs* (see p. 98) and get the children to mime the actions.

8 Singing Nursery Rhymes

Humpty Dumpty sat on a wall,
Humpty Dumpty had a great fall.
All the King's horses and all the King's men
Could not put Humpty together again.

Jack and Jill went up the hill
To fetch a pail of water,
Jack fell down and broke his crown
And Jill came tumbling after.

Ding dong dell, pussy's in the well.
Who put her in?
Little Tommy Thin.
Who pulled her out?
Little Tommy Stout.
What a naughty boy was that
To try to drown poor pussy cat
Who n'ere did any harm,
But killed all the mice in farmer's barn.

9   Two Little Dickie Birds—Fine Motor Dexterity

Enlighten the children about the secret of the two little dickie birds
(see Session V) and show them how they can play the same game
with their friends. Stick pieces of stamp paper on their index fingers
and carefully explain about changing the fingers when their hands
are behind their heads. When everyone has understood, act it out:

Two little dickie birds.
Sitting on a wall,
One named Peter,
One named Paul.
Fly away, Peter,   (Hands go behind head and fingers
Fly away, Paul,   change so that the middle
                                    finger is showing when the hands
                                    reappear, without any paper on.)

Come back, Peter,   (Hands go behind head again to
Come back, Paul.   change to index fingers, so that
                                    paper is visible again.)

10   Closing Activity—Ring a Ring of Roses

The children dance round in a circle, singing and ending by falling
down on the last line.

Ring a ring of roses,
A pocket full of posies.
Atishoo! Atishoo!
We all fall down.

Finale

Line up for Smarties, shake hands, and say Goodbye and Thank
you.

Materials required
Forty to fifty-piece wooden jigsaw puzzles.
Fishing rods with magnets on.
A box for a pond.
Cards of objects with a metal ring or clip attached to attract the
    magnet. Objects should contain a 'sh' or 'ch' sound in initial,
    medial or final position.
Micro cars.
Map of roads with lots of turnings.
Cowboys and Indians toys.

Concepts taught
Manual dexterity, awareness of space—jigsaw puzzles.
Fine motor dexterity, sound discrimination—fishing with magnets
    for cards.
Left, right orientation.
Finger play—*Peter Hammers with One Hammer*.
Question time.
Prepositions—with cowboys and Indians.
Story with actions.
Opposites.
Here We Go Round the Mulberry Bush.
Musical chairs.
Finale—social awareness.

1   Opening Activity—Manual Dexterity, Awareness of Space
Jigsaw puzzles—40–50 piece jigsaws. Mazes to find the way out
without going up any dead ends.

**2   Fishing with Magnets—Fine Motor Dexterity, Sound
    Discrimination**
Have a magnet for each child attached to a fishing rod. Inside a box
in the middle of the table have a number of cards with pictures of
objects having the sound 'sh' or 'ch' in initial, medial or final
position. Each card must have a metal staple or ring attached to it to
attract the magnet. When the child has caught a 'fish' he must name
it correctly in order to be able to keep it, otherwise it must go back in
the pond. The one with the biggest number of 'fishes' wins.

3 Left, Right Orientation
Draw a road with plenty of turnings and forks, then, using micro cars, ask each child in turn to 'drive' his car according to instructions.

4 Finger Play
Peter hammers with one hammer, one hammer, one hammer,
Peter hammers with one hammer all day long.
(hammer with one fist on the table)
Peter hammers with two hammers, etc.
(two fists on table)
Peter hammers with three hammers, etc.
(two fists and one foot)
Peter hammers with four hammers, etc.
(two fists and two feet)
Peter hammers with five hammers, etc.
(two fists, two feet and nodding head)
Peter's gone to sleep now, sleep now, sleep now,
Peter's gone to sleep now, all day long.
(put head on arms and pretend to be asleep)

5 Question Time
How many boys are there?
How many girls?
Hands up boys.
Hands up girls.
What colour is Jane/Tom's hair, jersey, trousers, shoes?
Are the boys dressed differently from the girls?
What difference is there?

6 Prepositions
Using cowboys and Indians and objects containing the sounds 'gr', 'br', 'gl'. Play the game as described in Session II.

7 Story with Acting
One morning the little Red Indian boy woke up,
    (yawn and stretch)
got out of bed and said to his mummy,
    (Oooooh! Oooooh—Indian war cry with first finger vibrating up and down in mouth)
'I'm going for a walk.'
He went down the garden path
    (walk with fingers)
and shut the gate.
    (clap hands)

He walked along the road till he came to a river.
He looked up the river and down the river,
    (look right and left)
but there was no bridge, so he swam.
    (make swimming movements)
When he got to the other side he found himself in a forest,
and he walked till he came to a big tree.
He looked round this side of the tree . . .
He looked round that side of the tree . . .
And what do you think he saw?
LIONS! (growling noises)
He turned and ran—back through the forest—swimming over the
river—running down the road—opening the gate—and into his
mother's arms (Oooooh! Oooooh!), doing all actions as fast as
possible on the return journey.

8   Opposites
First read out pairs of words which are opposite in meaning,
explaining them as you go, then play the game of opposites.

Stand *up*	(children stand)
Sit	(children supply word 'down' and suit the actions to these words)
Reach high	Reach . . . . (low)
Clap loud	Clap . . . . (soft)
Clap fast	Clap . . . . (slow)
Close your eyes	(open) . . . . your eyes
Pick up the book	Put the book . . . . . . (down)

9   Here We Go Round the Mulberry Bush
Here we go round the mulberry bush, the mulberry bush, the
    mulberry bush,
Here we go round the mulberry bush on a cold and frosty morning.
This is the way we clap our hands, clap our hands, clap our hands,
This is the way we clap our hands on a cold and frosty morning.
(Repeat with other actions.)

10   Musical Chairs
The children run clockwise round the room. When the music stops
they run to sit down—there being one chair less than the number of
children. The child with no chair is 'out' and another chair is
removed. The game continues until only one child is left.

Finale
Line up for Smarties, shake hands, and say Goodbye and Thank you.

Materials required
Beads for threading.
Cards of lemon, sugar, moon, sun, stone, cushion, man, boy,
　greyhound, snail, snow, coal.
Plurals lotto.
Cards with shapes where all are the same except one.

Concepts taught
Bead threading and sequencing.
Opposites.
Plurals—irregular.
Finger play—*Five Fat Gentlemen, Church and Steeple, Here's the
　Lady's Knives and Forks.*
Nursery rhymes—*Polly Put the Kettle On, Baa Baa Black Sheep,
　Hickory Dickory Dock, Humpty Dumpty, Jack and Jill.*
Odd man out—shapes.
Story—*The Three Little Pigs.*
Following instructions.
Finale—social awareness.

1　**Opening Activity**
Threading beads and copying shape sequences prepared by the
teacher.

2　**Opposites**
Present cards with the following pictures on them:
　　lemon　　　　sugar
　　moon　　　　sun
　　stone　　　　cushion
　　man　　　　　boy
　　greyhound　　snail
　　snow　　　　coal
explaining the opposite qualities of each pair. Then present the
questions orally:

Lemons are sour　　　　Sugar is . . . . . . ? (*sweet*)
The moon shines at night　The sun shines in the . . . . ? (*day*)
A stone is hard　　　　A cushion is . . . . . . ? (*soft*)

A man is tall   A boy is . . . . . . ? (*small*)
A greyhound is fast   A snail is . . . . . . ? (*slow*)
Snow is white   Coal is . . . . . . ? (*black*)

3   Plurals—Irregular
Played as a lotto game with singular and plural cards.

This time the teacher says, 'I have some teeth, who has one
. . . . . ?' and so on. Each child who responds accurately is given a
Smartie to put on his picture.

4   Finger Play 1
Five fat gentlemen standing in a row (*fingers held up straight*),
Five fat gentlemen bow down low (*bow with hands to head*),
Five fat gentlemen walk across the floor (*walk fingers across the
    table*),
Don't forget, gentlemen, please close the door (*clap*).

5   Finger Play 2
Here's the church
And here's the steeple.
Open the doors
And see all the people.
Here is the parson
Going up stairs,
And here he is in the pulpit
Saying his prayers.

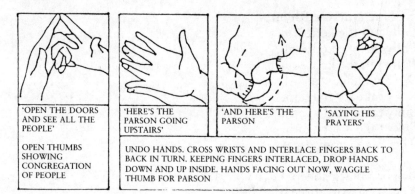

'OPEN THE DOORS AND SEE ALL THE PEOPLE' OPEN THUMBS SHOWING CONGREGATION OF PEOPLE	'HERE'S THE PARSON GOING UPSTAIRS'	'AND HERE'S THE PARSON	'SAYING HIS PRAYERS'
	UNDO HANDS. CROSS WRISTS AND INTERLACE FINGERS BACK TO BACK IN TURN. KEEPING FINGERS INTERLACED, DROP HANDS DOWN AND UP INSIDE. HANDS FACING OUT NOW, WAGGLE THUMB FOR PARSON		

6 Finger Play 3

Here's the lady's knives and forks
Here's the lady's table,
Here's the lady's looking glass
And here's the baby's cradle.
Rock! Rock! Rock! Rock!

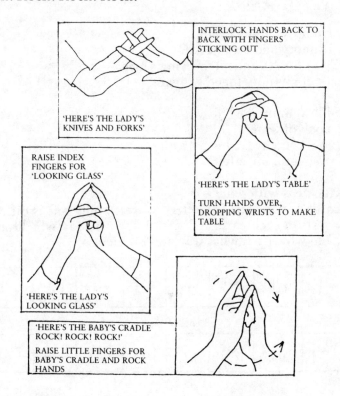

INTERLOCK HANDS BACK TO BACK WITH FINGERS STICKING OUT

'HERE'S THE LADY'S KNIVES AND FORKS'

RAISE INDEX FINGERS FOR 'LOOKING GLASS'

'HERE'S THE LADY'S TABLE'

TURN HANDS OVER, DROPPING WRISTS TO MAKE TABLE

'HERE'S THE LADY'S LOOKING GLASS'

'HERE'S THE BABY'S CRADLE ROCK! ROCK! ROCK!'

RAISE LITTLE FINGERS FOR BABY'S CRADLE AND ROCK HANDS

7   Sing Nursery Rhymes

Polly put the kettle on,
Polly put the kettle on,
Polly put the kettle on,
We'll all have tea.
Suky take it off again,
Suky take it off again,
Suky take it off again,
They've all gone away.

Baa baa black sheep, have you any wool?
Yes sir, yes sir, three bags full,
One for the master, one for the dame,
And one for the little boy who lives down the lane.

Hickory, dickory, dock,
The mouse ran up the clock,
The clock struck one,
The mouse ran down,
Hickory, dickory, dock.

Humpty Dumpty sat on a wall,
Humpty Dumpty had a great fall,
All the King's horses and all the King's men
Could not put Humpty together again.

Jack and Jill went up the hill
To fetch a pail of water,
Jack fell down and broke his crown
And Jill came tumbling after.

8   Which One is Different?

Present cards with a series of letters of which only one is different
from the rest on each card. Ask the children to say which one is
different and why, or in what way, it is different.

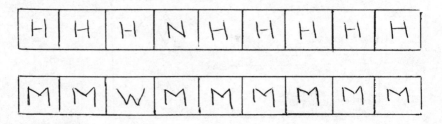

9 Listening to a Story

The Three Little Pigs (see p. 71)—the children joining in with 'I'll huff and I'll puff and I'll blow your house in,' etc.

10 Closing Activity

The children follow instructions given by the teacher. Then one of the children gives the instructions and the teacher joins in with those trying to follow them.

Finale

Line up for Smarties, shake hands, and say Goodbye and Thank you.

Materials required
Blocks—2.5 cms (one inch).
Pictures to colour in.
Picture cards of domestic items.
Wild and domestic animals.
Cards of odd man out—pictures.
Pictures to describe.
Tense cards—LDA or Philip and Tracey.
Plain paper and pencils.
What's wrong? picture, LDA.

Concepts taught
Building tower and bridge with blocks—manipulation.
Making a design with blocks.
Free drawing.
Prepositions using wild and domestic animals.
Odd man out—categorisation and rhyming.
Story—*Snow White and the Seven Dwarfs.*
Talk skills—describing pictures.
Tense, using cards.
Colour story—*Red Riding Hood.*
All Second Stage nursery rhymes.
Musical chairs.
Finale—social awareness.

1   Opening Activity—Ability to Manipulate Blocks
Building towers of blocks—note how many each child can balance.
Copying steps made of blocks.

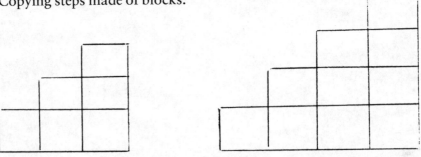

Make notes of the achievement of each child.

2   Drawing Test

Give each child a piece of plain paper and have him draw a man, a woman (Mummy), a child and a house. He can then colour them.

3   Categorisation and Prepositions

Using both wild and domestic animals, have the children sort them into their respective categories. Then ask each child which kind of animals he would prefer to have.

When he has a selection of animals, use the cards of domestic items and play the preposition game as before.

4   Odd Man Out—Categorisation—Rhyming

Which word does not rhyme? A lot of practice in rhyming will be necessary before this game can be played.

> Teacher says these words:
>   'hat   mat   cat   sit.'
> Which one does *not* rhyme?
> The children try to guess.
> Teacher says:
>   'sit   hit   hat   bit.'
> Which one does *not* rhyme?
> The children try to guess.
> Teacher says:
>   'cot   lot   not   slot.'
> Do all these rhyme?
> The children have to guess, and so on.

5   Listening and Memory

Snow White and the Seven Dwarfs (see p. 98). The children should be able to join in and answer questions about the story.

6   Talk Skills

What's wrong with this picture? Discussion to take place between teacher and children as to what is wrong and why.

7   Future Tense

We have been talking about the present tense and the past tense, now we will talk about the future tense—what is *going* to happen.

Teacher talks about this with the children till she feels they understand. Then she asks them to complete sentences like the following:

'I am washing these clothes now but by tomorrow I *will* have washed them.'

'In two years' time I . . . . be 8 years old.'
'My sister . . . . be going to University when she is 18.'
'Mummy and Daddy . . . . go to Spain next year for their holiday.'

8   Colour Story

Using the coloured blocks, give each child a selection. Each time a colour is mentioned in the following story, each child puts the right-coloured cube into the middle of the table.

One day, little *Red* Riding Hood went into the *green* forest. She was taking with her some food for her Grandma: a *yellow* wicker basket full of *red* apples, *brown* eggs and *green* beans, all wrapped in a *blue* napkin. Then out from behind a tree jumped a big *brown* wolf.

'Where are you going?' he asked little *Red* Riding Hood.

'I am going to see my Grandma,' she replied.

The wolf dashed off to the Grandma's cottage with the *blue* door and ate her up and got into her *pink* bed.

When little *Red* Riding Hood arrived, she looked at the big *brown* wolf and said, 'What big eyes you have, Grandma.'

And the wolf replied, 'All the better to see you with, my dear.'

Then *Red* Riding Hood said, 'What big teeth you have, Grandma.'

And the wolf replied, 'All the better to eat you with, my dear.'

He then jumped out of bed and tried to eat her. But she ran away and the huntsman in his *green* jacket came and shot the bad wolf.

9   Singing

All the Second Stage nursery rhymes (see p. 182).

10   Closing Activity—Gross Motor Co-ordination and Knowledge of Direction

Musical chairs, always going round clockwise.

Finale

Line up for Smarties, shake hands, and say Goodbye and Thank you.

Give the parents copies of all the Third Stage stories, nursery rhymes, songs and finger play rhymes for them to read to their children at home, and to practise ready for the next stage.

Materials required
Plain paper for drawing.
Paints or crayons for colouring.
Coloured beads and threading string.
Smallish box for each child.
Scissors for cutting out.
Paper for cutting out, pencils and rulers.
Mazes, taken from any Maze Book.
Number lotto.
A thimble.

Concepts taught
Free drawing and painting—the holidays.
Colour story.
Orientation—left and right.
Finger Play—*Five Little Soldiers.*
Discussion of roles—police.
Critical thinking.
Manual dexterity—origami (making things with paper and
   scissors).
Visual perception—mazes.
Number work—lotto.
Game—hunt the thimble.
Finale—social awareness.

1   **Opening Activity**
Free drawing and painting about the holidays. Then talk about the
holidays, saying what you did and encouraging the children to say
what they did.

2   **Colour Story**
Give each child a selection of coloured beads and have him put them
in a box in front of him. Each child needs a threading string. Say: 'I
am going to tell you a story, and in the story I shall name many
colours. When I say a colour, you hold up the bead which is that
colour. Then you thread it on your string.'

Ann and Bobby were going for a walk. Ann was wearing a black (*pause*) skirt and a white (*pause*) blouse. She had a red (*pause*) ribbon in her hair. Bobby wore green (*pause*) shorts and a yellow (*pause*) shirt. The blue (*pause*) sky and the white (*pause*) clouds made the children feel happy as they started on their walk. The sun was a yellow (*pause*) ball and made pretty patterns on the green (*pause*) leaves.

They walked down the path and into the wood where they saw a brown (*pause*) squirrel, a black (*pause*) butterfly with orange (*pause*) and purple (*pause*) spots, a skunk, all black (*pause*) with a white (*pause*) stripe, and a fuzzy caterpillar, yellow (*pause*) and grey (*pause*). They saw purple (*pause*) violets, white (*pause*) violets and yellow (*pause*) violets. A red-breasted (*pause*) robin flew over their heads and a yellow (*pause*) warbler sang hello. Ann and Bobby stopped to rest. They sat on the thick green (*pause*) grass and rested their heads on the trunk of a brown (*pause*) oak tree.

Ask each child to count how many green beads he has on his string, how many red beads, and so on.

3   Orientation—Identifying Right and Left
Follow these instructions given by the teacher.

Hold up your right hand.
Touch the person sitting next to you on the right.
Touch your right ear.
Bend your left elbow.
Touch your left eye.
Touch your right eye.
If this is your right arm, which is your right leg?
Touch your right leg with your left hand.
Put your right hand behind your back.
Put your left hand behind your back.

4   Finger Play
Five little soldiers

Standing in a row,

Three stood straight

And three stood so.

Along came the General

And what do you think?

Up jumped those soldiers

As quick as a wink.

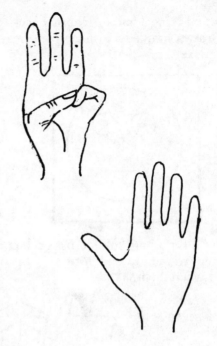

5 Talk Skills—Reasoning Ability

Show a picture of a policeman.

What does he do?

If you got lost in town, who would help you to get home?

Who keeps traffic moving in the city?

Who arrests people who do wrong?

Who helps us to know the right things to do?

If you are hurt, who will get help for you?

What do you think would happen if there were no policemen?

6 Critical Thinking Time

Ask the following questions and the children shout the answers.

Do you have four hands?

Does a fish have hands?

Does a fish have feet?

Does medicine taste better than Smarties?

What would you do if you found a wallet in the street?

What would you do if you saw smoke and fire coming from a
house?

Talk about all these things, such as the fact that monkeys have
four hands, and why. Fish don't have hands or feet but they have
fins—why? What are fishes' gills for?

7   Making a Sad or Happy Face—Manual Dexterity

Draw a simple face on a piece of paper about 5−8 cms (2−3 inches) square.

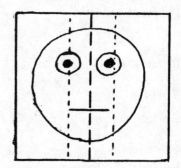

Put a mountain fold across each end of the mouth line and extend them to the top and bottom edges of the paper. Put a valley crease between them.

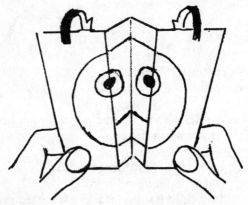

Hold the paper by the bottom corners and tilt the top edge towards you—the face will look sad.

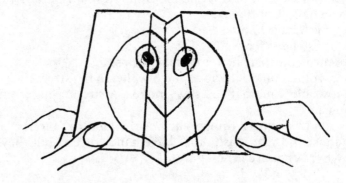

Tilt the bottom edge towards you and the face will look happy.

8   Visual Perception and Manual Dexterity
Using the photocopied sheets of mazes, have the children try to find their way out. They must not cross the lines or go along any 'dead ends'. Encourage them to *talk* about what they are doing and why.

9   Number Lotto
Play with singular and plural cards, as in Stage Two.

10   Hunt the Thimble
Play in the usual way. Hide the thimble and the children hunt for it. Tell them when they are getting 'warm' or 'cold'. The child who finds it can then hide it for the others to search for.

Finale
Line up for Smarties, shake hands, and say Goodbye and Thank you.

Materials required
Paper and scissors for cutting out.
Coloured beads and string.
Number lotto.

Concepts taught
Manual dexterity—origami.
Colour story.
Orientation—right and left.
Number lotto.
Number and action rhymes.
Nursery rhymes—*Pop Goes the Weasel, Georgie Porgie, Three Blind Mice, Hush-a-bye Baby, Jack and Jill, Hey Diddle Diddle.*
Story—*The Three Billy Goats Gruff.*
Game: *Looby Loo*—right, left reinforcement.
Acting with words—vocabulary building.
Hide and seek.
Finale—social awareness.

1   Opening Activity—Origami ('Fun with Paper')
Cutting out and making trees:

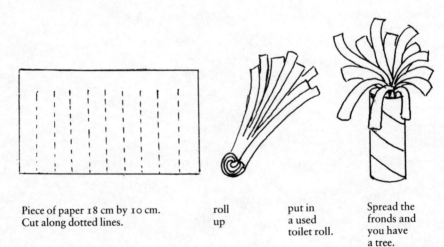

Piece of paper 18 cm by 10 cm.
Cut along dotted lines.

roll
up

put in
a used
toilet roll.

Spread the
fronds and
you have
a tree.

2 Colour Story

Using coloured beads, tell a story, with the children threading a bead of the right colour on a piece of string as colours are mentioned.

Tom had a *black* dog—his name was Rufus—and Rufus had a smart *red* collar. One day Tom was taking Rufus for a walk in the woods when they came to a clearing which was full of lovely flowers—*purple* crocuses, *yellow* daffodils, *white* snowdrops and *blue*bells. Suddenly a little *brown* rabbit came hopping along and Rufus couldn't resist chasing it and knocked all the flowers flat on the ground. Just then the keeper appeared in his *green* jacket and *grey* trousers, and when he saw all the flowers knocked down he was very angry. 'Clear off!' he shouted. Tom and Rufus didn't need to be told twice. They ran for their lives!

3 Orientation

Mark the children's hands with an 'L' and an 'R' if they are having trouble with Left and Right.

Simon says:
  Touch your right ear
  Touch your left ear
  Touch your right eye
  Touch your left eye
  Touch your right leg
  Touch your left leg.
  Stand up
  Raise your right leg
  Raise your left leg
  Turn round to the right
  Sit down.

4 Number Lotto

This time, when the children correctly identify the symbol with the correct number of objects, they have to write the number before they can keep the card.

5   Number and Action Rhyme
Five little soldiers

Standing in a row,

Three stood straight

And two stood so.

Along came the General

And what do you think?

Up jumped those soldiers

As quick as a wink.

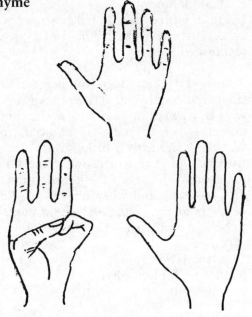

6   Nursery Rhymes
Half a pound of tuppenny rice,
Half a pound of treacle,
That's the way the money goes,
Pop goes the weasel!

Georgie Porgie pudding and pie
Kissed the girls and made them cry,
When the boys came out to play,
Georgie Porgie ran away.

Three blind mice, three blind mice,
See how they run, see how they run,
They all run after the farmer's wife,
Who cut off their tails with a carving knife,
Did you ever see such a thing in your life,
As three blind mice.

Hush-a-bye baby on the tree top,
When the wind blows the cradle will rock,
When the bough breaks the cradle will fall,
Down will come cradle, baby and all.

Jack and Jill went up the hill
To fetch a pail of water
Jack fell down and broke his crown
And Jill came tumbling after.
Up Jack got and home did trot
As fast as he could caper,
Went to bed to mend his head
With vinegar and brown paper.

Hey diddle diddle,
The cat and the fiddle,
The cow jumped over the moon,
The little dog laughed
To see such fun
And the dish ran away with the spoon.

7 Listening and Joining In

Play the story *The Three Billy Goats Gruff* on the tape recorder. The children to listen and join in with the more familiar repetitive parts.

THE THREE BILLY GOATS GRUFF

Once upon a time there were three Billy Goats called Gruff. There was a great big Billy Goat Gruff, a middle-sized Billy Goat Gruff and a little baby Billy Goat Gruff.

One day they decided to go up on the hillside across the river to eat grass and grow fat. The first one to start along the road was little baby Billy Goat Gruff. Soon he came to a bridge. Now, under this bridge there lived a mean old giant, with eyes as BIG as saucers and a nose as LONG as a poker. When he heard the little baby Billy Goat Gruff going trip trip trip over his bridge, he growled, 'Who is that tripping over my bridge?'

'It is I,' said little baby Billy Goat Gruff. 'I am going up on the hillside to eat grass and grow fat.'

'Oh no, you're not,' said the old giant. 'I am coming up there to eat you up.'

'Please don't do that,' said baby Billy Goat Gruff. 'Wait and eat middle-sized Billy Goat Gruff who will be coming along soon. He is much bigger and more tender than I am.'

'Very well, be off with you, then,' said the old giant. So the little baby Billy Goat Gruff hurried on up the hillside to eat grass and grow fat.

After a little while the middle-sized Billy Goat Gruff came to the same bridge. When the old giant heard him going trip-trap, trip-trap over his bridge, he growled, 'Who is that trip-trapping over my bridge now?'

'It is I,' said the middle-sized Billy Goat Gruff. 'I'm going up on the hillside to eat grass and grow fat.'

'Oh! no, you're not,' said the old giant. 'I am coming up there to eat you up.'

'Please don't do that,' said the middle-sized Billy Goat Gruff. 'Wait and eat the big Billy Goat Gruff who will be coming along soon. He is much bigger and more tender than I am.'

'Very well, be off with you, then.' So the middle-sized Billy Goat Gruff hurried on up the hillside to eat grass and grow fat.

After quite a while, the great big Billy Goat Gruff came to the same bridge. He was very big. When he started over the bridge, it seemed as if it might break. Trop, trop, trop he went.

'Who is that tropping over my bridge?' growled the old giant.

'WHO ARE YOU THAT WANTS TO KNOW?' said the great big Billy Goat Gruff.

'I am the old giant who lives under this bridge, and I am coming up there to eat you up,' answered the old giant.

'ALL RIGHT, COME ALONG, THEN,' said the great big Billy Goat Gruff. The old giant came up on the bridge. Suddenly the great big Billy Goat Gruff rushed at him, tossing him high in the air. The big, bad giant came down in the water, and sank to the very bottom of the river. He was never seen again. Then the great big Billy Goat Gruff went up on the hillside to eat grass and grow fat along with the other two billy goats.

8   Reinforcement of Knowledge of Left and Right

Here we go looby loo,
Here we go looby light,
Here we go looby loo,
All on a Saturday night.
You put your right foot in,
You put your right foot out,
You put your right foot in,
And shake it all about,
You do the hokey cokey and turn around,
And that's what it's all about.
Repeat with: left leg in and out,
            right arm in and out,
            left arm in and out.

9 Acting Out

Ask the children to act the meaning of these commonly used words, to improve vocabulary:

    Upside down
    Sideways
    Backwards
    Over
    Through
    Top
    Bottom

Then use the words in context, each child in turn making up a sentence with one of these words in it.

10 Closing Activity—Hide and Seek

One child is chosen as 'he'. The other children turn their backs, close their eyes and count to 20. They turn round and seek the child that is hidden. Each child should have a chance to be 'he'.

Finale

Line up for Smarties, shake hands, and say Goodbye and Thank you.

STAGE THREE
SESSION III

Materials required
Paper and scissors.
Logiblocks—squares and circles, some thin, some thick, some large
   some small.
A thimble.
Star chart and stick-on stars.

Concepts taught
Origami—manual dexterity and vocabulary.
Riddles.
Comparison of adjectives.
Sequencing.
Colour.
Nursery rhymes.
Story—*Snow White and the Seven Dwarfs.*
Hunt the thimble.
Here we go looby loo.
Musical chairs.
Finale—social awareness.

1 Opening Activity—Origami
Fun with paper and scissors: making snakes.

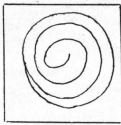  

Draw a coil on a piece of paper 6″ square (15 cm). | Decorate with spots and eyes and cut round, starting with the tail. | Glue the tail to another piece of paper. Add a tongue.

Make the snake rear up making a hissing sound.
Everyone tries to think of words beginning with 's'.

2 Riddles—What Am I?
The teacher asks the questions and the children guess the answers.

I am small,
I am furry,
I wash myself with my tongue,
I say 'Meow'.
    What am I?
I have a round face,
I have two hands,
I say tick tock.
    What am I?
I can hop,
I have two long ears,
I like to eat lettuce leaves.
    What am I?
I have big wings,
I fly in the air,
People ride in me.
    What am I?

Then mime the different objects and have the children guess from this what they are. The children then have a turn to mime the objects while everyone else guesses.

3   Comparison of Adjectives

Make a pile of Logiblocks for each child (only squares and circles, but thick, thin, large and small). Examine them and see their attributes. Ask each child in turn:

Give me a thick one.
Give me a thin one.
Give me a round one.
Give me a square one.
Give me a large one.
Give me a small one.

Then ask each child about the blocks he has left: 'What kind of blocks have you got?'
    Each child selects one of his blocks and is then asked:
    'Is yours thicker than Tommy's?'
    'Is yours bigger than Sue's?'
        and so on.

4   Sequencing

Give out all the blocks equally.
    The teacher makes a sequence of blocks and then covers it and

asks the children to make it from memory. Successful attempts are given a star on their chart (see last page of this session).

5   Colour and Counting

Ask the children to count their blocks and then return the blocks by colour—give me the blue one, the red one, etc.

6   Nursery Rhymes

Half a pound of tuppenny rice,
Half a pound of treacle,
That's the way the money goes,
Pop goes the weasel!

Georgie Porgie pudding and pie,
Kissed the girls and made them cry,
When the boys came out to play,
Georgie Porgie ran away.

Three blind mice, three blind mice,
See how they run, see how they run,
They all run after the farmer's wife,
Who cut off their tails with a carving knife,
Did you ever see such a thing in your life,
As three blind mice.

Hush-a-bye baby on the tree top,
When the wind blows the cradle will rock,
When the bough breaks the cradle will fall,
Down will come cradle, baby and all.

Jack and Jill went up the hill
To fetch a pail of water
Jack fell down and broke his crown
And Jill came tumbling after.
Up Jack got and home did trot
As fast as he could caper,
Went to bed to mend his head
With vinegar and brown paper.

Hey diddle diddle,
The cat and the fiddle,
The cow jumped over the moon,

The little dog laughed
To see such fun
And the dish ran away with the spoon.

7   Story
Read *Snow White and the Seven Dwarfs* (see p. 98).

8   Hunt the Thimble
Play as before.

9   Here We Go Looby Loo
Here we go looby loo,
Here we go looby light,
Here we go looby loo,
All on a Saturday night.
You put your right hand in,
You put your right hand out,
You put your right hand in,
And shake it all about,
You do the hokey cokey and turn around,
And that's what it's all about.
Repeat with left hand, right and left foot.

10   Musical Chairs
Play as before.

Finale
Line up for Smarties, shake hands, and say Goodbye and Thank
you.

STAR CHART

NAME	DATE	DATE	DATE	DATE	DATE

Materials required
Photocopied sheets of mazes of varying difficulty.
Logiblocks.
Shape Lotto.
Small objects and a tray for Kim's game.
Cards with pictures of different objects.
Wooden or plastic numbers.

Concepts taught
Mazes.
Riddles.
Comparison of adjectives—greater than, smaller than.
Story—*Snow White and the Seven Dwarfs*.
What's missing?—Kim's game.
Talk skills.
Acting and guessing—charades.
Ordering of numbers.
Classification: odd man out—listening skills.
Game—*Oranges and Lemons*.
Finale—social awareness.

1 **Opening Activity—Mazes**
Have ready some photocopied mazes of varying difficulty from a
maze book. Start with the easy ones and then give more and more
difficult ones to the children who have managed the easy ones. It
will be necessary to explain that the child should try not to cross the
lines and make sure each one understands what is meant by a 'dead
end'. (See overleaf for sample mazes.)

2 **Riddles**
I am big,
I wag my tail,
I am brown,
I say bow-wow.
  What am I?
Usually I'm made of leather,
You wear me on your feet,

I keep them warm and dry.
    What am I?
I am big and grey and strong,
I have big ears and a long trunk.
    What am I?
I stand on four legs,
I live in the bedroom,
You sleep in me.
    What am I?
I live on the farm,
I eat grass,
I give you milk,
I say moo.
    What am I?

3   Comparison of Adjectives
Use cards of different sized shapes:
Two to start with,
    then three,

then four.
Which is the largest?
Which is the smallest?
What are the shapes called?
Match them to Logiblocks.

Play Lotto with shapes so that the card turned over must match exactly the shape on the child's card—small circle to small circle, big circle to big circle, and so on.

4   Story
Read *Snow White and the Seven Dwarfs* (see p. 98).

5   Kim's Game
Memorising objects on a tray, and then saying what has been taken away.

6   Object Cards of All Kinds of Things to Discuss
What are they used for?
Have you got one at home?
Would you like one?
    and so on.

7   Who Am I Talking About and What Am I
Using the characters from *Snow White and the Seven Dwarfs*, act each character and have the children guess which one you are supposed to be. Ask each child to tell a part of the story.

8   Ordering of Numbers
Use wooden or plastic numbers 1 to 9. First lay them out in order and count them with the children, placing a finger on each number as you do so.

Then muddle them up and ask each child to arrange them in order again.

9   Classification or Odd Man Out—Listening Skills
Ask each child to say which word does not belong in the following series. Give two examples to ensure that they understand what is required.

Examples:
    red, green, blue, hat.
'Hat' is the odd one—discuss the reason why 'hat' does not belong with the others.

Now try out another set:
cat, dog, mitten, rabbit.
Again explain that 'cat', 'dog' and 'rabbit' are all animals, while 'mitten' is clothing. So 'mitten' is the odd one.

Now ask each child to say which is the 'odd man out' of these series:
boat, car, man, wagon
orange, bell, pear, apple
chair, carrots, potatoes, onions
table, chair, desk, sun
sun, moon, star, flower
dress, shirt, skirt, car.

10 Closing Activity—Oranges and Lemons

The teacher and the tallest child make the arch while the other children line up to make a ring, passing under the arch as they dance round in a circle.

Oranges and lemons, say the bells of St Clements.
You owe me five farthings, say the bells of St Martins.
When will you pay me? say the bells of Old Bailey.
When I grow rich, say the bells of Shoreditch.
When will that be? say the bells of Stepney.
I do not know, says the great bell of Bow.
Here comes the candle to light you to bed,
Here comes the chopper to chop off your head.
Chop, chop, chop, chop.

The arms of the people making the arch then come down, trapping one child. The child then joins one of the two arch people. The next child is allocated to the other side. When all children have been caught and lined up behind their leader, a tug of war takes place, usually ending in everyone falling on the floor.

Finale

Line up for Smarties, shake hands, and say Goodbye and Thank you.

Materials required
More advanced wooden jigsaw puzzles.
Alphabet Bingo—counters.
Paper and pencils for drawing.
Cards with different combinations of numbers on them.
Tiddlywink counters.
What's wrong picture—the street.
Star chart and stick-on stars.

Concepts taught
Visual perception—more advanced wooden puzzles.
Classification—seeing or hearing.
Alphabet bingo—capital letters.
Conversation time—wishes.
Relationships.
Parts of the body song.
Story—*The Hare and the Tortoise.*
Number bingo.
Number rhymes.
What's wrong with this picture?—the street.
Game—*Oranges and Lemons.*
Finale.

1 **Opening Activity—Visual Perception**
Using the more advanced wooden puzzles, discuss with the children
why the straight-sided pieces should go round the outside and why
this pink piece should go next to another pink piece, and so on.

2 **Classification**
Do you *see* or *hear* these things?
    Radio playing
    Stop sign—or bus stop sign
    Music playing
    Whispering voices
    Lovely yellow flowers
    Dog barking
    Numbers on a blackboard

Fire engine siren
A new red shirt.
What else can you see or hear?

Alphabet Bingo—Capital Letters

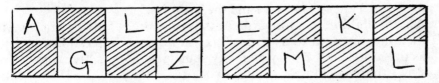

The teacher calls out a letter—the child covers it with a counter if it is on his card.

A card with different letters must be made for each child.

3   Conversation Time
Ask each child what he would wish for if a fairy godmother said he could have just one wish. The children can then draw their wish if it is something that can be drawn.

4   Relationships
Snow is cold
Fire is . . . . . . (*hot*).
(*Discussion: How you know fire is hot.*)
Sand is dry.
Water is . . . . . . (*wet*).
The sun shines in the day.
The moon shines at . . . . . . (*night*).
People walk.
Birds . . . . . . (*fly*).
A dog is an animal.
An apple is a . . . . . . (*fruit*).
A snail is slow.
A rabbit is . . . . . . (*fast*).
A tree is a plant.
A chair is . . . . . . (*furniture*).
See if the children can think of some for themselves.

5   Activity Song
With parts of the body to tune of *There is a Tavern in the Town, in the Town*:

My head, my shoulders, knees and toes, knees and toes,

My head, my shoulders, knees and toes, knees and toes,
My eyes, my ears, my mouth, my nose, my mouth, my nose,
My head, my shoulders, knees and toes, knees and toes.

Touch each part of the body as it is said.

6   Story Time—The Hare and the Tortoise

Ask the children questions about the story afterwards, to improve
their memory and comprehension. Ask inferential questions, such
as the moral of the story and why some people do better who are
slower but take more care, and so on.

THE HARE AND THE TORTOISE

Once upon a time a hare met a tortoise on a road that led to a pretty
little town. 'Good morning, friend Tortoise,' said the Hare. 'Where
are you going this fine day?'

'I'm going to the river that flows through the pretty little town,'
replied the Tortoise.

'That is a long way off for someone who travels as slowly as you
do,' said the Hare. 'If you could run as fast as I can, you would soon
be there.'

'I know I am slow,' replied the Tortoise, 'but at that, I might win a
race from you.'

The very idea of running a race with the Tortoise made the Hare
laugh and laugh. But at last he said, 'I think it might be fun to run a
race with you.'

They asked the Fox to be the judge of their race, and when they
were ready, the Fox said, 'One, two, three—go.'

Upon hearing the word 'go', away they went. With a leap and a
bound, the Hare was soon out of sight of the Tortoise. When he was
about halfway to the river, he thought, 'That Tortoise will never
catch up with me. There is no need to hurry any more. I shall rest
here for a few moments.' So he nibbled a little grass and sniffed
about in a nearby clover field. Then he lay down and was soon
asleep. After a time the Tortoise passed the sleeping Hare. He did
not stop to look at him but kept moving steadily onwards until he
came to the river. When the Hare woke up the Tortoise was
nowhere in sight. 'The Tortoise is certainly a slow creature,' said the
Hare, and wandered on down to the river. When he got there the
Tortoise was waiting for him with the Fox sitting beside him.

'Well! well!' said the Fox. 'Leaps and bounds do not always win a
race. Slow and steady won this one.'

7   Number Bingo

Matching spoken symbols to written symbols. This is played like the adult form of bingo, where a number is called out by the teacher (from 1 to 20) and the child covers it with a tiddlywink if he has it on his card. The child to complete his card first calls out 'Bingo.' The teacher needs to keep a record of the numbers called so that the child's card can be checked. He needs to be able to name the numbers that are covered on his card in order to win.

8   Number Rhymes

One, two, three, four, five,
Once I caught a fish alive,
Six, seven, eight, nine, ten,
Then I let it go again.
Why did you let it go?
Because it bit my finger so.
Which finger did it bite?
This little finger on the right.

One, two, buckle my shoe,
Three, four, knock at the door,
Five, six, pick up sticks,
Seven, eight, lay them straight,
Nine, ten, a big fat hen.

9   What's Wrong with this Picture?

Show children the 'What's Wrong?' picture of the street (see overleaf). Each correct response earns a star (see last page of session for star chart). There are 36 possible things that they can spot as being wrong. The picture should be coloured in before you start, so that traffic lights can be shown in the wrong order and street signs can be incorrectly coloured.

Discussion should then follow as to why it is wrong and what would happen if things were really like that—a square wheel, the canopy upside down, a picture on the wall of the house instead of a window, and so on.

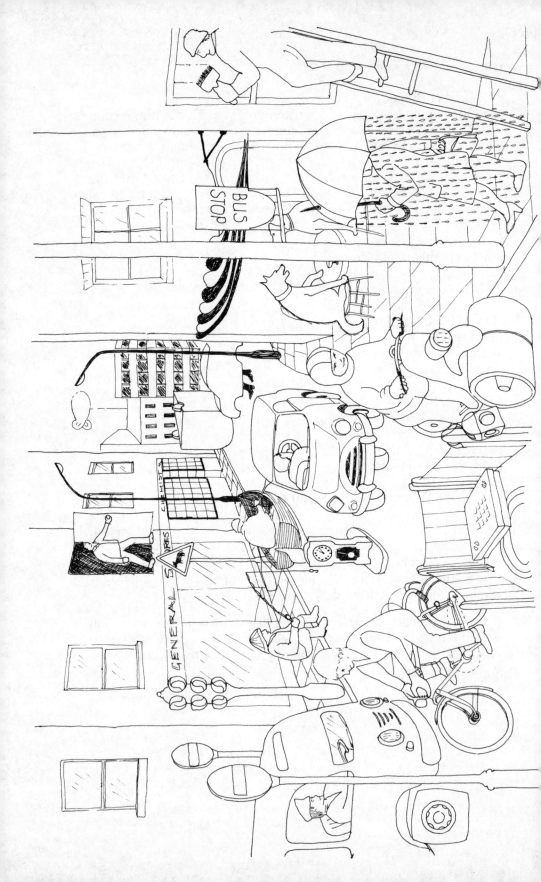

10 Oranges and Lemons
Played as in Session IV.

Oranges and lemons, say the bells of St Clement's.
You owe me five farthings, say the bells of St Martin's.
When will you pay me? say the bells of Old Bailey.
When I grow rich, say the bells of Shoreditch.
When will that be? say the bells of Stepney.
I do not know, says the great bell of Bow.
Here comes the candle to light you to bed,
Here comes the chopper to chop off your head.
Chop, chop, chop, chop!

Finale
Line up for Smarties, shake hands, and say Goodbye and Thank
you.

STAR CHART

NAME	DATE	DATE	DATE	DATE	DATE

STAGE THREE
SESSION VI

Materials required
Plasticine.
Model of an alphabet rainbow.
Alphabet bingo—lower case letters; counters.
Wooden or plastic numbers.
Star chart, and stick-on stars.
Two vowel cards 'ă' and 'ŏ'.
Pairs game of 'ă' and 'ŏ' words.

Concepts taught
Plasticine modelling—making the capital letters.
Listening, rhyming and memory.
Parts of the body—more advanced.
Alphabet bingo—lower case letters.
Riddles: What am I?—parts of the body.
Number relay race.
Auditory discrimination—short vowels, 'ă', 'ŏ'.
Matching pictures to words—pairs games.
Miming opposites.
Game—*Old Macdonald Had a Farm.*
Finale—social awareness.

1   Opening Activity
Plasticine modelling of the capital letters, as many as each child can
manage. A large model of an alphabet rainbow should be in sight
(see overleaf).

2   Listening, Rhyming and Memory
Hands used with appropriate actions.
>Hands can lift a box or chair.
>Hands can toss things in the air.
>Hands can sweep the kitchen floor.
>Hands can open the front door.
>Hands can cut and paint and draw.
>Hands can carry, clap and saw.
>Hands can lead rhythm bands.
>   What can *you* do with your hands?

Children then say what *their* hands can do, and also try to
remember what the poem said about hands.

ABCDEFGHIJK L MNOPQRSTUVWXYZ

Legs
Eight on a spider.
Six on a flea.
Four on an elephant.
But only two on me.
Discuss the difference between a spider and an insect and why
spiders have eight legs.

3   Alphabet Bingo—Lower Case Letters

g		t		c		i
n	k	z		r		
v		e		x	a	p

o		b		m		f
s	l		u		q	
j		d		w	h	y

Explain the difference between capital (big letters) and lower case
(small letters) and when you use them.

Children cover the letters with counters as they are called out.
They are asked to check their cards if they have called bingo, by
pointing to each letter as it is named by the teacher.

4   Parts of the Body—More Obscure Features
Simon says: touch your—

head	eyelashes	lips	elbow
hair	eyelids	teeth	wrist

ears	nose	tongue	hands
eyes	nostrils	shoulders	fingers
eyebrows	mouth	arms	fingernails
knees	legs	foot	toes
			toenails.

5   Riddles—What Am I?

I help you see.
I help you throw a ball.
I help you hear.
I help you kick a ball.
You have five of me on each hand.
I help keep water or dust out of your eyes.
I help you bite food.
You have five of me on each foot.
I bend when you touch your head.
I help you smell.
I bend when you walk upstairs.
I help you talk.
I help you breathe.

6   Number Relay Race

Have two sets of wooden or plastic numbers laid out randomly on two tables at one end of the room. Divide the children into two teams and have them stand at the opposite end of the room. Give the one, two, three, go, signal. Each child runs to the table, picks up the number 1, runs back and hands it to the next child who runs and picks up number 2, and so on till all the numbers have been collected. If a child brings the wrong number back, it has to be returned and the next child takes over.

7   Auditory Discrimination

What sounds do you hear in these words? Is it an 'ŏ' or an 'ă'? Have two cards on the table with a letter and a picture on them. One should have 'a' for apple and the other 'o' for orange (the pictures should be coloured). See overleaf for sample cards.

cot	cap	bat	pot
top	mat	fan	hot
log	map	strap	shop
dog	frog	can	man

8   Matching Pictures to Words

Using the words in the previous activity have cards with the pictures drawn on them and another set of cards with the words on them which have the vowel on the reverse side (see opposite and p. 160).

Play this as a pairs card game. The child first turns over a blank card which has the picture on the other side. He then decides whether the object has an ŏ in the middle or an ă. If he decides it is an ŏ he looks for a card with ŏ on it and turns it over. If the word thus revealed matches the picture he has made a pair and keeps it. If not, both cards are turned face down and the next child has a turn. It is important to remember where the cards are if they have not been paired.

A blank card is always turned over first.

SHORT VOWEL PAIRS GAME

Cards should be cut up and mixed around. Picture cards should be face down—vowel cards should be word down and the vowels showing on the reverse side.

o	a	a	o
o	a	a	o
o	a	a	o
a	a	o	o

9 Miming Opposites
Teacher mimes the following and each child has to mime the opposite.
Teacher mimes:

Sad	Child mimes . . . . . . (*happy*)
Cross	Child mimes . . . . . . (*pleased*)
Nice	Child mimes . . . . . . (*nasty*)
High	Child mimes . . . . . . (*low*)
Fat	Child mimes . . . . . . (*thin*)
Fast	Child mimes . . . . . . (*slow*)
Pretty	Child mimes . . . . . . (*ugly*).

Now try verbal opposites:
   These apples are cheap, those are . . . . . . ?
   This path is crooked, that one is . . . . . . ?
   My knife is sharp, Tommy's is . . . . . . ?
   Mother has a loud voice, Granny has a . . . . . . ?
   Hedgehogs are prickly, a baby's skin is . . . . . . ?
   My skirt is tight, but Mary's is . . . . . . ?
   He is an ugly man, but his brother is . . . . . . ?

10 Closing Activity
All the children join in singing *Old Macdonald Had a Farm*, making
the appropriate animal noises each time a new animal is introduced.
Because all the previous animals are repeated each time a new verse is
sung, this is a good test of memory.

Old Macdonald had a farm, e-i-e-i-o,
And on that farm he had some ducks, e-i-e-i-o,
With a quack-quack here
And a quack-quack there,
Here a quack, there a quack,
Everywhere a quack-quack,
Old Macdonald had a farm, e-i-e-i-o.

Old Macdonald had a farm, e-i-e-i-o,
And on that farm he had some pigs, e-i-e-i-o,
With an oink-oink here
And an oink-oink there,
Here an oink, there an oink,
Everywhere an oink-oink,
A quack-quack here,
And a quack-quack there,
Here a quack, there a quack,
Everywhere a quack-quack,
Old Macdonald had a farm, e-i-e-i-o.
(*Continue as above, adding new animals with each verse: lambs—
baa-baa; turkey—gobble-gobble; dog—woof-woof; cows—moo-
moo; cat—meow-meow, etc.*)

Finale
Line up for Smarties, shake hands, and say Goodbye and Thank you.

STAGE THREE
SESSION VII

Materials required
Galt's wooden capital letters.
Model of alphabet rainbow, as in Session VI.
Paper with faintly drawn capital letters, for tracing.
Paper faintly arranged as a rainbow, for tracing.
Alphabet bingo—lower case letters and counters for covering the
    letters.
Sheets of faintly drawn numbers for children to trace.

Concepts taught
Laying out the alphabet—capitals.
Tracing the alphabet.
Learning to write—from the top.
Naming parts of the body.
Story—*The Hare and the Tortoise.*
Alphabet bingo—lower case letters.
Picking out letters when named.
Nursery songs—*Sing a Song of Sixpence, Little Bo Peep, Three
    Blind Mice.*
Nursery rhymes—*Gorgie Porgie, Hush-a-bye Baby, Jack and Jill,
    Hey Diddle Diddle.*
Work on rhyming.
Number rhymes—*Once I Caught a Fish Alive, One, Two, Buckle
    My Shoe, Ten Green Bottles.*
Tracing over numbers.
Old Macdonald Had a Farm.
Finale—social awareness.

1   **Opening Activity—Laying Out the Alphabet**
Give the children sets of Galt's wooden capital letters. A large model
of the alphabet rainbow should be on the table in front of the
children for them to copy (see p. 156).

2   **Tracing Over the Alphabet Rainbow**
Provide paper already prepared with faintly drawn capital letters.
Remind the children that ALL LETTERS start from the TOP.
Before any writing activity takes place ask the children:

'And where do all letters (or numbers) start?'
Children shout the response: 'FROM THE TOP!'
If there is any problem over this, mark the starting point with a red dot.

3 Parts of the Body
Teacher touches the following parts of her body and the children have to say what she is touching:

eyelashes	eyebrows	lips	ears
eyes	nose	mouth	neck
shoulders	elbows	knees	ankles
teeth	fingernails	wrist	tongue
			hair.

Now discuss with the children by asking them what each part of their body is for, and what you would find difficult if you did not have that part, or it was not working properly.

4 Story—The Hare and the Tortoise
Children to narrate a part of the story in turn (see story, p. 150).
Prompt each child with: 'And what happened then?'

5 Alphabet Bingo—Lower Case Letters
Play as described in Session VI (see p. 156).

6 Nursery Songs
Sing a song of sixpence,
A pocket full of rye,
Four and twenty blackbirds
Baked in a pie,
When the pie was opened
The birds began to sing,
Wasn't that a funny dish to set before a King?

The king was in his counting house
Counting out his money,
The Queen was in the parlour
Eating bread and honey,
The maid was in the garden
Hanging out the clothes,
When down came a blackbird
And pecked off her nose.

Little Bo-Peep has lost her sheep
And doesn't know where to find them,
Leave them alone and they will come home,
Bringing their tails behind them.
Then up she took her little crook,
Determined for to find them,
She found them indeed but it made her heart bleed
For they'd left their tails behind them.

Three blind mice, three blind mice,
See how they run, see how they run,
They all run after the farmer's wife,
Who cut off their tails with a carving knife,
Did you ever see such a thing in your life,
As three blind mice.

7   Nursery Rhymes

Georgie Porgie Pudding and Pie,
Kissed the girls and made them cry,
When the boys came out to play,
Georgie Porgie ran away.

Hush-a-bye baby on the tree top,
When the wind blows the cradle will rock,
When the bough breaks the cradle will fall,
Down will come baby cradle and all.

Jack and Jill went up the hill
To fetch a pail of water,
Jack fell down and broke his crown
And Jill came tumbling after.
Up Jack got and home did trot
As fast as he could caper,
Went to bed to mend his head
With vinegar and brown paper.

Hey diddle diddle, the cat and the fiddle,
The cow jumped over the moon,
The little dog laughed to see such sport
And the dish ran away with the spoon.

    Discuss which words rhyme. See if the children can think of other
words that rhyme with 'hill', 'top', 'pie', 'sheep' and so on. 'Diddle'

is more difficult, but some children might manage 'middle', 'twiddle', 'fiddle', if they are given one or two clues. Miming clues are always permitted to trigger off the required response.

8 Number Rhymes with Actions

One, two, three, four, five,
(count on fingers)
Once I caught a fish alive,
Six, seven, eight, nine, ten,
(count on fingers of the other hand)
Then I let it go again.
(now the children are holding up ten fingers)
Why did you let it go?
Because it bit my finger so.
(shake right hand and grimace as though hurt)
Which finger did it bite?
This little finger on the right.
(hold up the little finger on the right hand).

One, two, buckle my shoe,
(pretend to do up shoe)
Three, four, knock at the door,
(make two knocks on the table)
Five, six, pick up sticks,
(pretend to pick up sticks)
Seven, eight, lay them straight,
(pretend to lay them straight)
Nine, ten, a big fat hen.
(make a big circle with arms to show the fat hen).

Ten green bottles standing on the wall,
(hold up both hands with all fingers extended)
Ten green bottles standing on the wall,
But if one green bottle should accidentally fall,
(bend one finger down over the palm)
There'll be nine green bottles standing on the wall.

Nine green bottles standing on the wall,
(hold up both hands with nine fingers extended)
Nine green bottles standing on the wall,
But if one green bottle should accidentally fall,
(bend another finger down over the palm)
There'll be eight green bottles standing on the wall.

(Continue as above until both hands have all fingers bent.)

9   Tracing Over Numbers

Ask the children to trace over the numbers already drawn faintly on sheets of paper. Do not forget to ask:

'Where do *all* numbers *start*?'
Response: 'FROM THE TOP!'

10   Old Macdonald Had a Farm

Sing *Old Macdonald Had a Farm* (see p. 161), with the children making the appropriate animal noises in each verse.

Finale

Line up for Smarties, shake hands, and say Goodbye and Thank you.

Materials required
Rainbow alphabet to colour in—one for each child.
Chart of rainbow alphabet with consonants green, vowels red, and
  'y' coloured half red and half green. Crayons for colouring.
Two sets of wooden alphabet letters (made by Galt)
Star chart, and stick-on stars.
A set of wooden or plastic numbers for each child.
Cards with the numbers written on them.
Set of domestic animals in families.
Cards of objects beginning with consonant blends 'thr', 'sw', 'scr'
  'shr' 'spl' 'str' 'spr' 'sp' 'st' 'skw' (squ).

Concepts taught
Colouring in alphabet letters—recognition of vowels.
Singing the Vowel Song.
Alphabet relay race.
Finger play rhyme—*Church and Steeple.*
Ordering numbers one to nine in reverse.
Copying numbers—ordering, saying and writing.
Tongue twisters—articulation and pronunciation.
Prepositions and animal families and initial consonant blends.
Story—*The Three Billy Goats Gruff.*
Dancing and singing the Vowel Song.
Finale—social awareness.

1 **Opening Activity**
Colour in alphabet letters—consonants green, vowels red, with the
part-time vowel 'y' coloured half red and half green. (See p. 168 for
rainbow.)
  A chart will have to be prepared and fixed to the wall as a guide
for the children to follow with the correct colouring of the letters.
Some will even need to copy from a model beside them, which will
need to be the same size as their own colouring sheet.

2 **Singing the Vowel Song (see p. 169 for tune)**
a   e   i o u,
Without one of these no word can you do,
But if that word should end in 'i',

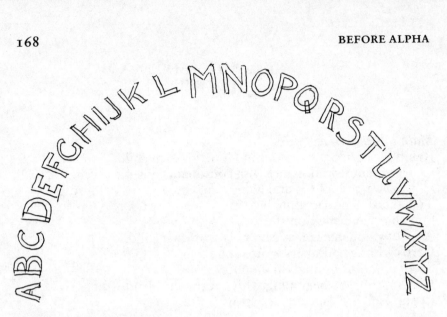

Then you must change the 'i' to 'y'.
WHY? (*all shout together*)
Because . . .
No English word ends in 'i',
No English word ends in 'i'.

3   Alphabet Relay Race

Divide the children into two groups. Spread two sets of Galt's alphabet letters on two tables at the other end of the room, in a sequential arc. The children run, one at a time, to the table, pick up the first letter and run back to hand it to the next child in their team, saying THE NAME OF THE LETTER as they do so. If any child fails to name the letter he must return it to the table and the next child runs to pick it up.

The first team to complete the alphabet wins and has a star put on the team's star chart (see last page of session).

4   Finger Play Rhymes—done sitting down

Here is the church,
  (*interlace fingers with knuckles showing upwards*)
Here is the steeple,
  (*point index fingers up together to make a steeple*)
Open the doors,
  (*turn hands over with fingers still interlaced*)
And here are the people.
  (*wriggle fingers*)
Here's the parson going upstairs,

(make a ladder with left hand, walk right thumb and index finger up the ladder)
Here he is in the pulpit saying his prayers.
(show thumb protruding from hole made by index finger and thumb of the opposite hand).

Repeat until all the children have mastered the words and the movements.

5 Ordering Numbers in Reverse Order

Hand each child a set of wooden or plastic numbers. Time them to see how many seconds each one takes to arrange them from 9 down to 1. Now have each child *say* the numbers, first forwards and then backwards.

Now have them *write* the numbers, first forwards and then backwards, *saying* the numbers as they write them.

Do not forget your drill:
Teacher: 'Where do numbers start?'
Children: 'From THE TOP!'

Have ready some cards with the numbers written on them for the children to copy if they are having difficulty writing them spontaneously.

6 Tongue Twisters

This is to improve articulation and precision of pronunciation of words. Exercises of this nature are excellent for helping children to pronounce words properly when they are working out the sounds for spelling.

She sells sea shells on the sea shore,
But the shells that she sells are not shells, I'm sure.

Peter Piper picked a peck of pickled pepper.
If Peter Piper picked a peck of pickled pepper,
Where is the pickled pepper Peter Piper picked?

How much wood would a woodchuck chuck
If a woodchuck could chuck wood?
A woodchuck would chuck as much wood
As a woodchuck would chuck if a woodchuck could chuck wood.

Fuzzy Wuzzy was a bear,
Fuzzy Wuzzy had no hair,
So Fuzzy Wuzzy wasn't fuzzy, wuzzy?

Number rhymes (see p. 165)
Repeat until all children can say them properly.

One, two, three, four, five,
Once I caught a fish alive.
etc.

One, two, buckle my shoe,
Three, four, knock at the door.
etc.

Ten green bottles standing on the wall.

7   Prepositions
—'forwards', 'sideways', 'backwards', 'upside down'.
Using a selection of toy animals which come in families—male,
female, offspring—sort the toys into their families:

Bull, cow, calf. Stallion, mare, foal. Pig, sow, piglets. Dog, bitch,
puppy. Tom cat, cat, kitten. Cock, hen, chicks.

Have a pack of cards of objects starting with the consonant blends:

Three 'thr'	Swan 'sw'	Screw 'skr'	Shrimp 'shr'
splash 'spl'	strap 'str'	spring 'spr'	spray 'spr'
split 'spl'	spiral 'sp'	staircase 'st'	square 'skw'

Go through the cards, asking each child what the picture is and
what sound the word starts with. The teacher should say the sound
first and the children repeat it after her.

Then give a card to each child, who should have an animal family
in front of him, and ask him to place the 'strap' or whatever beside
his animals and then to move the 'stallion' 'towards' the 'strap'; the
'mare' 'sideways' towards the 'strap'; the 'foal' 'upside down'
beside the 'strap'.

Go through each animal family with each child in the same way,
bringing in all the prepositions denoting spatial relationships. Then
ask each child to give you the 'stallion, mare, foal', saying where
each one is in relation to the card beside it. Finally, call for the cards,
asking the child to give the beginning sound for each object.

8   Consonants Story
Tell the following story, asking the children to shout when they hear
the sounds that they have just been practising. If possible, they
should shout the relevant sound.

*Three sw*ans landed on the lake with a *spl*ash and ate the *shr*imps
that *spr*ang up all around in a *sp*iral *spr*ay.

They *spl*it up and formed a *sw*an *squ*are with a *scr*ew at each corner to hold it down!

9   Story—The Three Billy Goats Gruff

It is some time since they heard this story (see p. 135), so before beginning see how many children can remember what it was all about.

Then read the story with the children being encouraged to join in—especially with the dialogue, using the appropriate voices. Have them say it *with* you—for example, Mean old giant *growling*, 'Who is that tripping over my bridge?' Baby Goat in *squeaky* voice, 'It is I, I am going up the hillside to eat grass and grow fat', and so on.

10   Closing Activity

Dance around the room singing the Vowel Song.

Finale

Line up for Smarties, shake hands, and say Goodbye and Thank you.

STAR CHART

NAME	DATE	DATE	DATE	DATE	DATE

STAGE THREE
SESSION IX

Materials required
Sheets of alphabet tracking.
Alphabet bingo—lower case letters.
Paper and pencils.
Story—*The Three Billy Goats Gruff* on tape.
Coloured bricks.
Pictures of objects with something missing.

Concepts taught
Alphabet tracking.
Vowel Song.
Alphabet bingo—lower case and naming letters.
Writing own first name.
Action rhyme—*There is a Tall Shop*.
Story on tape—*The Three Billy Goats Gruff*.
Writing numbers spontaneously.
Making steps from cubes.
What is missing?
Singing alphabet.
Finale—social awareness.

1 Opening Activity
Alphabet tracking as far as 'n' (see overleaf).

The child should cross off each letter of the alphabet with a red crayon as he comes to it. He should say the *alphabet aloud* as he crosses off each letter.

The children may need some help with this activity to begin with. Continue until you are sure each child has fully understood. Then give them another sheet to complete on their own.

2 Singing the Vowel Song
Sing to the tune given on p. 169.

a   e   i   o   u,
Without one of these no word can you do,
But if that word should end in 'i',
Then you must change the 'i' to 'y'.
WHY? (*All shouted together*)

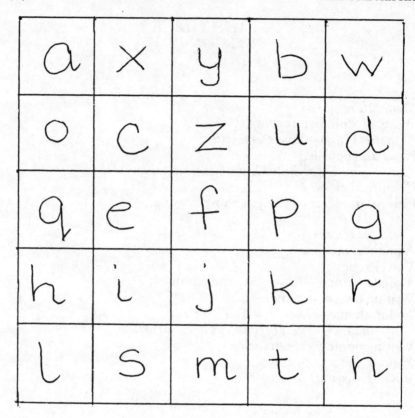

Because...
No English words ends in 'i',
No English words ends in 'i'.

3 Alphabet Bingo—Lower Case Letters
The children should now be able to *name* the letters as their card is
checked and they hand in their cards.

4 Learning to Write their First Name
First the children trace over the letters you have written faintly, then
copy them, saying the *names* of the letters as they write them.
Remember the drill:
   'Where do the letters start?'
   'At the TOP!'
   Make sure that the body of each letter sits on the line and that the
ascenders and descenders do not go above or below the line by more
than ⅓ of the body size—thus:

abcdefghijklmnopqrstuvwxyz

Always have the alphabet written like this at the top of every page when the children are expected to write anything.

5 Action Rhyme

There is a tall shop in the town,
   (Use arms to make a roof over head)
Lifts moving up and down,
   (Move clenched fists up and down in opposite directions)
Doors swinging round about,
   (Move fists round each other)
People walking in and out.
   (Move fists forwards and backwards crossing each other)

Repeat two or three times

6 Story on Tape

Play *The Three Billy Goats Gruff* on tape, with the children listening, then play it again with children joining in. Finally, have the children act the parts as well as say them in conjunction with the taped story.

7 Writing Numbers Spontaneously

Ask the children to write the numbers 1 to 9, then to match each number to the correct number of coloured bricks which are in a pile in the middle of the table.

8 Making Steps From Cubes

First copying from a model made by the teacher, then making steps by themselves. Finish by building as tall a tower as possible. On a given signal they all blow their towers down.

9 What is Missing From These Pictures?

10 Singing the Alphabet
The children dance round the room, singing the letters of the alphabet to a favourite tune.

Finale
Line up for Smarties, shake hands, and say Goodbye and Thank you.

STAGE THREE
SESSION X

Materials required
Vowel tracking sheets.
Chart of alphabet with vowels in red, and semi-vowel 'y' half red
   and half green. Consonants should be green.
Galt's wooden alphabet letters or plastic letters—lower case.
Vowel chart.
Cards with the following words written on them:

cat	hat	mat	sat
wet	let	set	pet
hit	lit	sit	pit
pot	cot	hot	lot
mut	cut	hut	rut

Alpha to Omega flashcards.
Star chart and stick-on stars.

Concepts taught
Vowel tracking.
Extracts from all the stories.
Alphabet rainbow—picking out the vowels.
Making words.
Singing all the songs.
Saying all the nursery rhymes.
Writing the alphabet to dictation.
Alpha to Omega flashcards of letters and sounds.
Dancing and singing the Vowel Song.
Finale—social awareness.

1   Opening Activities
Vowel tracking (see overleaf).
   The child is to cross off each vowel as he comes to it, saying the
names of the letters as he crosses them off.
   The vowels should include the semi-vowel 'y' and a chart should
be prepared for each child to have in front of him (see overleaf).
   Help the children to do this until you are sure everyone has
understood, then give them a fresh tracking sheet to do on their
own.

x	p	a	t	e
s	i	z	o	q
u	r	a	m	l
e	k	y	i	b
d	o	f	h	u

2   Stories

Read extracts from each of the stories that the children have heard
throughout the three Stages and have them guess which story each
extract came from:

a)   'Mirror, mirror on the wall, who is fairest of them all?'
b)   The Fox said, 'One, two, three, go!'
c)   'Oh no, you're not, because I'm coming up there to eat you up!'

d) 'Who's been sitting in my chair and broken it all to pieces?'
e) 'I shall build a stronger house than yours.'

Now discuss all the stories and any morals and values that they might be depicting, also going into the more generalised whys and wherefores. For example:

'Think of other ways in which people who are too quick and sure of themselves might not always be the winners.'
'Why was the Queen so jealous of Snow White?'
'Can jealousy be a bad thing?'
'If so, why?'
'What lesson did Goldilocks learn?'
'Does the baddy usually come to a bad end?'
'Why was the third little pig's house better than all the others?'
'What was wrong with the other houses?'

3 Laying Out the Alphabet in a Rainbow—Lower Case

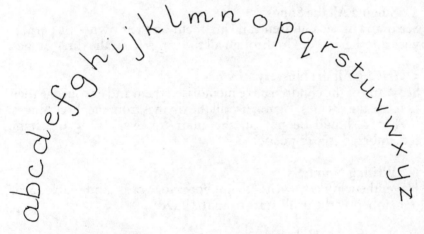

Use Galt's wooden alphabet letters or plastic letters. Pick out the vowels—just 'a', 'e', 'i', 'o', 'u'—from the rainbow.

Taking one vowel at a time, see if the children can make the following words with the letters of the alphabet when you sound it out for them. The ending will always be the same, so they only have to alter the initial letter.

cat	hat	mat	sat	vowel 'ă'
wet	set	let	pet	vowel 'ĕ'
hit	sit	lit	pit	vowel 'ĭ'
pot	cot	hot	lot	vowel 'ŏ'
mut	cut	hut	rut	vowel 'ŭ'

Make sure the child replaces the letter in the correct position in the alphabet rainbow after he has made each word.

When you change vowels, draw the children's attention to the new vowel's sound. Point out the new vowel on the vowel chart (see p. 178), which should be in front of them, so that they fully realise the change in sound.

Finally, give each child a card with the words written on it and ask each one to read the words. If they find this difficult, sound it out for them thus:

c – at	h – at	m – at	s – at
w – et	l – et	s – et	p – et
h – it	l – it	s – it	p – it
p – ot	c – ot	h – ot	l – ot
m – ut	c – ut	h – ut	r – ut

Ask them to push these sounds together to make a word.

4 Singing All the Songs
See if any of the children can sing them on their own—or perhaps with another child. Go through all the songs from the three Stages.

5 Saying All the Nursery Rhymes
See if any of the children have memorised them and encourage them to recite the rhymes. Again, use all the rhymes from the three Stages.

A star should be put on the chart for every song or rhyme remembered (see opposite).

6 Writing Numbers
Have the children write them both forwards and backwards, remembering the drill: start from the TOP!

7 Writing the Alphabet
Writing the alphabet to dictation, remembering the drill. Dictate it in names.

8 Go Through the Alpha to Omega Flashcards
Use only the cards of single letters at this stage, presenting them thus:

Show the *letter* card—children say the *name*.

Turn it over so that the picture is revealed.

Children say the *name* of the *picture*.

Teacher asks what the first *sound* is.

Children give the *sound* of the letter.

9   Skipping Round the Room
First hopping—first on one foot then on the other. Then catching a large sponge ball while saying the alphabet. The teacher stands in the middle and throws the ball to each child in turn as she says the first letter, the child says the next letter as he throws the ball back, the teacher then says the next letter while throwing the ball to the next child, and so on until the alphabet has been completed.

10   Dancing Round the Room Singing the Vowel Song
See p. 169 for the Vowel Song tune.

Finale
Tea party with small iced cakes to mark the end of the programme. Each child to be given a balloon or carnival novelty as a prize.

STAR CHART

NAME	DATE	DATE	DATE	DATE	DATE

SUMMARY OF STORIES AND RHYMES

Stage One

Story	Goldilocks and the Three Bears
Nursery Rhymes	Polly, Put the Kettle On
	Baa Baa Black Sheep
	Oh Dear, What Can the Matter Be?
Action Rhymes	The Farmer's in his Den
	This is the Way We Wash Our Face
Finger Play Rhymes	Ten Little Men
	I Am a Teapot

Stage Two

Stories	The Three Little Pigs
	Snow White and the Seven Dwarfs
Nursery Rhymes	Humpty Dumpty
	Hickory, Dickory Dock
	Ding Dong Dell
	Jack and Jill
Action Rhymes	Here We Go Looby Loo
	Here We Go Round the Mulberry Bush
	Ring a Ring of Roses
Finger Play Rhymes	Incy Wincy Spider
	Two Little Dicky Birds
	Five Little Soldiers
	Five Fat Gentlemen
	Here's the Lady's Knives and Forks
	Church and Steeple
	Peter Hammers with One Hammer
Number Rhyme	One, Two, Buckle My Shoe

Stage Three

Stories	The Three Billy Goats Gruff
	The Hare and the Tortoise
Nursery Rhymes	Sing a Song of Sixpence
	Little Bo-Peep
	Pop Goes the Weasel
	Georgie Porgie
	Three Blind Mice

	Hush-a-Bye, Baby
	Hey Diddle Diddle
Action Rhymes	Oranges and Lemons
	There is a Tall Shop
	Old Macdonald Had a Farm
Number Rhymes	Once I Caught a Fish Alive
	Ten Green Bottles
Tongue Twisters	She Sells Sea Shells on the Sea Shore
	How Much Wood would a Woodchuck Chuck
	Peter Piper Picked a Peck of Pickled Pepper
	Fuzzy Wuzzy Was a Bear

NOTE

Several of the rhymes and stories appear in more than one Stage, and the rhymes are repeated cumulatively at the end of each Stage, but they are listed here in the Stage in which they first appear.

USEFUL BOOKS AND MATERIALS

Branches of Childsplay and the Early Learning Centre
Games and books:
Fisher Price Tape recorder
Tempo talking stories and poems
Pickwick Tell-a-Tale tapes in association with Ladybird Books
Party games and songs tape
Percussion instruments and other musical instruments
Magnetic fish pond
Picture Pairs
Tongue Twisters cassette and matching game
Snap cards
Picture Lotto
Nursery rhyme puzzles
My Room wooden puzzle
Noah's Ark puzzle
Match and Make Farm Animals puzzles
House Puzzle
Farmyard wooden puzzle
Clock jigsaw
Number teaching jigsaw
Mosaic wooden puzzle
Wooden bricks (drum of 100)
Other square wooden blocks (2.5 cms)
Farm animals
Doll's house furniture
Stacking and nesting toys
Logic I Launching logic shapes

General
Ladybird Play Books
The Pooh Painting Book, Methuen Children's Books
Dot-to-Dot books
Mazes books
Make Your Own Pop-Ups, by Joan Irvine, Angus & Robertson
Tricks and Games with Paper, by Paul Jackson, Angus & Robertson
Alpha to Omega Flashcards, by Bevé Hornsby, Heinemann Educational Books
Plasticine

Boxes of spent matches
Drinking straws
Round and Round the Garden: Play rhymes for young children,
    by Sarah Williams, Oxford University Press
Ready for School (Six titles). Invader Limited (1986), 10 Eastgate
    Square, Chichester
ESM Software for Schools (1988 catalogue), Duke Street,
    Wisbech, Cambs PE13 2AE. (Tel: 0945 63441)

LDA Wisbech, Cambs PE13 2AE
Listen and Do tapes
Set of Pattern Blocks
Pattern Blocks activity book
Look! Hear! Tapes and photographs for matching sounds to
    pictures
Wotami? Tape of 16 sounds and a living creature to identify
Visual Discrimination Activity booklets
Visual Recall Flashcards of shapes and objects
Extendable Card Holder
Sequential Thinking Cards
Time and growth sequencing cards
Pictures, please! 1,232 line drawings for making games
Self adhesive teaching pictures
Early language stamps
What's wrong cards
What's wrong posters
Special Software—pre-reading
Soft vinyl triangular pencil grips
Minimal match—letter/sound lotto set
Phonic stamps 1 and 2.

Taskmaster
Set attribute dominoes—connecting similar features
Think a Link—association pictures
Square Stamp for making 10 cm by 10 cm squares
Shopping games
Money dominoes
Coloured cubes for cognitive skills
Sequencing beads and 60 cm laces
Pegboard designs
Shapes stamps
Zip top wallets for storing cards and games
Seasonal sequence cards

ESA
Educational Supply Association Ltd, Harlow, Essex.
Everyday pictures
    The Street—people who work for us
                the vehicles
    The Country and Seaside—in the country
                    by the sea
    The Home—furniture
             domestic utensils

Pictures for Discussion
Postcards obtainable from any art gallery of paintings by famous artists, such as:

L. S. Lowry, Sir John Everett Millais, John Constable, Francis Davis Millet, Thomas Weaver, J. M. W. Turner, Philip Wilson Steer, Sir David Wilkie, Sir Lawrence Alma-Tadema, Henry Thomas Alken, Sir Edwin Landseer, William Logsdail, etc.

Choose paintings with plenty of things going on, and which clearly depict the artist's style.

TESTING YOUR CHILD'S PROGRESS

Now that your child is ready for school, how much will he benefit from his education?

The following simple tests will indicate where difficulties still lie and what aspects of development still need help.

COPYING SHAPES TEST

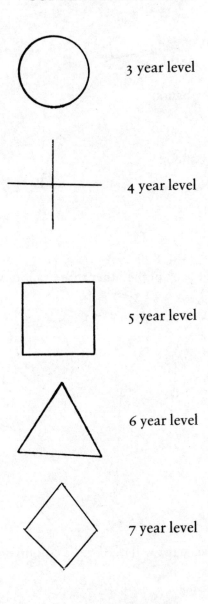

3 year level

4 year level

5 year level

6 year level

7 year level

KNOWLEDGE OF COLOURS

Recognition: 4 year level
Show me the red balloon

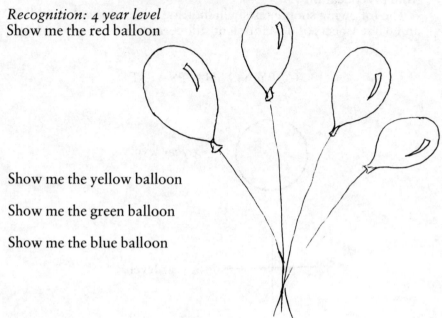

Show me the yellow balloon

Show me the green balloon

Show me the blue balloon

Naming: 5 year level
What is the colour of this balloon?
Repeat question for each of the other three balloons.

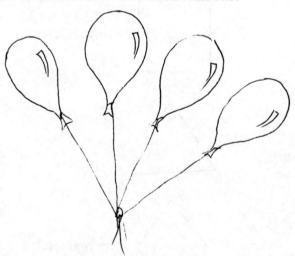

The balloons on this page will need to be coloured before showing them to the child.

ORAL LANGUAGE TEST
5 Year Level

Cards I to VIII
Progressive Use of Plurals

Card I
Say to the child, 'Here is one ball.'

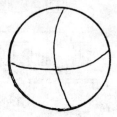

Card II
Say, 'Here are four . . . . . . ?'

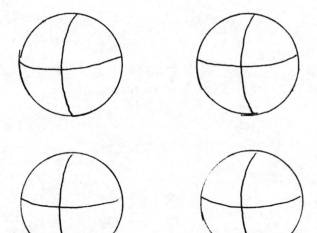

(Colour the balls as children respond better to colour.)

Card III
Say to the child, 'Here is one house.'

Card IV
Say, 'Now here are three . . . . . . ?'

(Colour the houses as children respond better to colour.)

Card V
'Here is one mouse.'

Card VI
'Here are two . . . . . . ?'

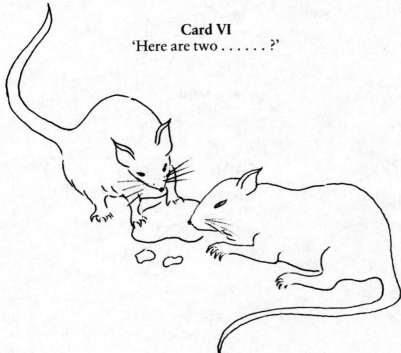

(Colour the mice and the cheese.)

Card VII
'Here is one goose.'

Card VIII
'Here are three . . . . . . ?'

(Colour the beaks and legs of the geese yellow.)

Card IX
Naming of Shapes

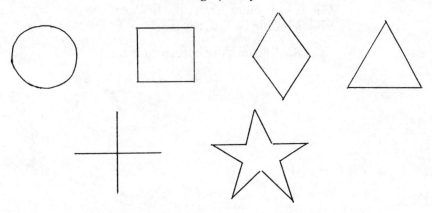

Card X

1) Relationships.   2) Causality.   3) Opposites.   4) Time.

1   a)   What do you do when you are tired?
   b)   Tell me some things that fly.
2   a)   What should you do before you cross the road?
   b)   Why do you do this?
3   a)   Brother is a boy, sister is a . . . .
   b)   Father is a man, mother is a . . . . .
   c)   In the day it is light, at night it is . . . .
4   a)   Is it morning or afternoon?
   b)   What season is it?

Card XI
Describing a Picture (see overleaf)

Question 1   Tell me everything you can see in this picture.
            Prompt with, 'Is that all you see? What is this?'
Question 2   Tell me what they are all doing?
            Prompt, 'What is the father doing?' etc.
Question 3   How many dogs are there?
            How many children are there?
            How many grown-ups are there?
Question 4   What colour is the father's jersey?
            What colour is the boy's jersey?

What colour is the girl's jersey?

Question 5   Who is standing on the bridge?

Who is swimming under the bridge?

Who is hiding behind the tree?

Colour picture before you start.

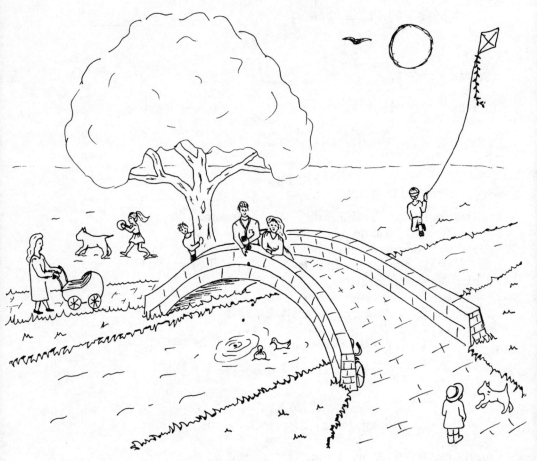

Card XII
Concept Formation and Following Instructions

Materials required
Nest of boxes of different colours.
Coloured wooden beads; some round, some oval.

Colour
Instructions:
1 Sort the beads into their colours and put them into the box of the same colour.

Shape and pronouns
Instructions:
2 The yellow box is yours, the blue box is 'mine'—now put all the *round* beads into 'your' box and all the *egg shaped* beads into 'mine'.

Position
3 a) Put the white box on top of the yellow box.
  b) Put the green box underneath the blue box.
  c) Put the white box inside the yellow box.

Heavy and Light
  Is the yellow box heavier or lighter than the blue box?

Large and Small
  Have I got a few beads in the blue box, or many beads?
  Repeat with opposite number of beads in box.

Number
  How many red beads are there? (have nine in the box).

MOTOR DEVELOPMENT TEST

4 year level. Movements may first be demonstrated
1 *Balance*
   Standing with one foot in front of the other for fifteen seconds, eyes open.
2 *Knowledge of limbs in space*
   Touch point of nose with index finger, first right and then left, eyes closed.
3 *Gross movement*
   Hop in the same place, feet together, seven times.
4 *Speed—fine movement*
   Put 20 coins in box in fifteen seconds.
5 *Simultaneous movement*
   Describe circles with index fingers, arms extended at sides for ten seconds.
6 *Associated movements*
   To clasp your hand with his right hand and then his left, then both together, without moving other parts of the body.

5 year level
1 *Balance*
   To balance on tip toe for ten seconds, eyes open.
2 Knowledge of limbs in space. Roll up a piece of paper into a ball, eyes closed.
3 *Gross Movement*
   To hop on one foot for five metres.
4 *Speed—fine movement*
   To put 20 matches in a box, one by one, ten with each hand, in 20 seconds.
5 *Simultaneous movement*
   Tap head and rub tummy.
6 *Associated movement*
   Lick round lips—first clockwise then anti-clockwise, without grimacing.

APPENDIX
FOR TEACHERS AND
THERAPISTS

GENERAL DEVELOPMENT IN YOUNG CHILDREN

A child's level of intelligence (which is partly inherited and partly influenced by home and surroundings) has a profound effect on his development. Children with mental handicap are late in all aspects of development, except perhaps sitting and walking. They show less interest in their surroundings, are less responsive, less alert and lack concentration.

The intelligent child, however, is more advanced in development with the possible exception of sitting and walking: he is more alert, interested and responsive to his environment.

The following pages chart the developmental stages through which most children pass between the ages of two and five. Some will reach these stages more quickly, others more slowly, but they provide a general guide to average progress.

Two Years

Posture and large movements
Balance almost complete.
Runs, stops, starts and dodges things.
Kicks a ball without falling.
Usually squats when playing on the floor.
Can go up and down stairs two feet to a step.
Becoming agile and climbs a great deal.
Climbing frame useful.
Very inquisitive so home safety is important.

Vision and fine movements
Becoming increasingly controlled.
Can undo things, like sweets.
Can make a tower of six to seven bricks.
Loves looking at books and being read to.
Turns pages of book singly.
Can recognise familiar adults in pictures.
Can imitate mother drawing a vertical stroke or circle.
Turns door knobs and can unscrew things.

Speech and hearing
Has at least 50 words and can have up to 200.

Two or three word phrases developing.
Constant questions, mostly asking for names of things.
Can pick out eyes, hands, feet, etc., even from pictures.
Beginning to develop inner language.
Starts to use pronouns, 'I', 'you', 'me', 'mine'.
Good idea of plurality.
Syntax less good.
Beginning to have some concept of time.
Starts relating things that have happened.
Jargon almost gone, but still telescopes phrases.
Initial and final consonants fairly accurate, medials less so.
Lots of repetitions and hesitations.
Asks for drink, food, lavatory.

Behaviour and play
Starting to be independent, but when tired or frightened, still clings
    to mother.
Suffers very much if separated from mother for any reason.
Still finds it difficult to share things and does not play with other
    children but likes to play on his own in their presence.
Tends to develop jealousy.
Washes and dries hands.
Puts on shoes, socks, pants; takes them off.
Dry at night if lifted.
Beginning of simple make-believe play: putting doll to bed, making
    tea, etc.
Gives first name.
Uses spoon competently.
Drinks without spilling.
Talks continuously to himself during play.
Water play very popular.

Two and a Half Years

Posture and large movements
Similar to two-year-old but more advanced.
Likes simple nursery apparatus, such as slides, etc.
Can now jump with two feet.
Can stand on one foot and kick a ball.
Can also stand on tiptoe.

Vision and fine movements
Can pick up needle and thread with one eye shut.

Can balance eight bricks.
Can draw.
Can recognise own picture.
Can thread wooden beads.
Knows one colour.

Speech and hearing
Still a certain amount of echolalia (repeating what is said to him).
Vocabulary of 200 to 300 words.
Very keen to tell you things, sometimes stuttering with eagerness.
Knows own whole name.
Talks to himself a great deal.
Words 'Yes' and 'No' have been internalised and child can use them
    to regulate own behaviour.
Still some telescoping.
Pitch more stable.
Occasional mastery of initial consonant blends.
Medials still not always accurate.

Behaviour and play
Fully toilet trained in day and usually at night if woken once to use
    the potty.
Can attend to toilet needs except wiping.
Can dress and undress himself.
Can eat well with spoon and possibly fork as well.
Very inquisitive and independent and therefore rebellious.
Less easy to distract him from frustrations.
Still dependent on the proximity of an adult.
Imagination developing.
Plays with dolls and cars.
Watches older children with great interest.
Will share toys for short periods.

Three years

Posture and large movements
Stands on preferred foot for a second or two.
Goes upstairs with alternating feet.
Downstairs two feet to a step.
Jumps off the bottom step with both feet.
Can ride a tricycle.
Likes pulling toys.
Can now hop and walk a few steps on tip-toe.

Vision and fine movements
Can manipulate small objects with ease.
Can balance nine to ten bricks and can copy a bridge of three cubes
    from model if shown how.
Can draw V T H O from a model.

Can draw a man, sometimes with an arm or leg missing.

Can match primary colours, particularly red and yellow.
Blue and green are more difficult.
Can use scissors.

Speech and hearing
Very large vocabulary—up to 1,000 words.
Use of pronouns not fully mastered.
Knows own whole name and sex.
Imagination very well developed.
Long monologues and meaningless chants.
Multiplicity of questions.
Can hold a conversation.
Can be reasoned with.
Can carry out complicated orders with relationships.
Loves stories and likes favourites over and over again.
Knows some nursery rhymes.
Counts to ten.
Beginning to offer linguistic rather than physical resistance.
Medials still sometimes omitted or substituted.
Still telescoping.
Still some repetition of phrases.
Blends becoming mastered.
Some reversal of syllables.

Behaviour and play
Developing table manners.
Uses fork and spoon well.
Can wash and dry own hands.
Fully toilet trained by day and night.
Can dress fully except shoelaces.
Can share toys and sweets.
Can take part in group activities and understands about taking
    turns.
Needs other children to play with.
Likes helping with simple activities at home.

Can think of others as well as himself.
Will show affection for a new baby.

Four Years

Posture and large movements
Balance nearly complete.
Can bend down to pick things up with straight legs.
Can balance on one foot for ten seconds.
Can hop on one foot.
Can skip on one foot.
Goes downstairs one foot per step.
Can rotate index fingers, arms extended.
Can bring fingers in to touch nose, eyes closed.

Vision and fine movements
Even greater precision with small objects.
Can put 20 small coins into a box in 20 seconds.
Can manage clockwork toys.
Can imitate fine finger movements without any synkenesis (associated body movements such as wiggling tongue or the other hand not being used).
Can draw V I H T O X A from a model.
Man now has a hat, hands and feet:

Can now match all four primary colours and sometimes name them.
Can build three steps with six cubes after demonstration or from a model.

Speech and hearing
Articulation almost complete but sometimes 'r' and 'w' are confused, as well as 'y' and 'l', and 'd' and 'th'.
Memory more developed.
Knows name, age, sex and address.
This is the peak question period, particularly 'why' and 'how'.
Still likes to listen to stories, but also likes to tell them, tending to confuse fact and fiction.
Speech used more and more to control others.
Questions and statements are an expression of the intricate abstract patterns which he is learning to employ as he achieves command of relationships between persons, objects, situations and activities.

Critical to the point of embarrassment.
Most medials correct.
Voice more subdued.
Repetitions sharply reduced.
Still a few reversals of syllables.

Behaviour and play
Can wash himself.
Can clean own teeth.
Really needs other children to play with but tends to be aggressive.
Often has imaginary friends.
Begins to be impertinent, but understands reasons for doing and not
    doing things.
Can dress and undress except ties for boys and laces.

Five years

Posture and large movements
Can balance on one foot with arms folded for five to ten seconds.
Can skip on alternate feet.
Can hop on both right and left feet.
Can ride a bicycle.
Can swim.
Knows left and right on himself but not on others until age seven.

Vision and fine movement
Can draw ○ + ☐ △ (from model for triangle).
Can copy all capital letters and write some spontaneously.
Can draw:

Can write simple words, and own first name.
Can write numbers from 1–9.
Can count objects to ten and sometimes to 20.
Can name four colours and match up to 12.
Can tie shoe laces.

Speech and hearing
Speech fluent.
Vocabulary of between 1,500 and 2,000 words.
Syntax correct.

Gaining information by asking questions but fewer and more relevant.
Can make definitions, e.g. horse to ride, apple to eat.
Has ear as well as eye for detail.
Can appreciate rhythm and rhyme.
Can recite poems and sing nursery rhymes.
Can recall events of the day.
Knows name, age, address, sex and birthday.

Behaviour and play
Is now capable of being independent.
May still have imaginary friends.
Likes dressing up.
Learns to cheat so needs to be taught about rules of fair play.
Likes collecting things.
Quarrelsome and competitive.
Can manage knife and fork.
Can bath himself.
More sensible and controlled.
Chooses own friends and knows the reason.
Is now ready for formal education.

THE HORNSBY AUDITORY DISCRIMINATION, REPETITION AND SPELLING ABILITY TEST

Introduction

This test will be useful to speech therapists, psychologists and medical practitioners to aid diagnosis of difficulties in perception, discrimination and reproduction, both spoken and written, of word forms.

The results could form the basis for treatment techniques, highlighting both weaknesses and strengths.

The test aims to investigate six aspects considered to be necessary prerequisites for the acquisition of spelling skills:

1 The ability to perceive differences in pairs of words when spoken by the examiner (interpersonal speech discrimination).
2 The ability to repeat accurately the words presented.
3 The ability to monitor *personal* speech at the level required for the phoneme/grapheme translation involved in spelling (intrapersonal speech discrimination).
4 The ability to translate minimal phonemic differences between words into written symbols.
5 The ability to hold in mind the auditory pattern and sequence of the words in order to reproduce them on paper.
6 To tap the child's knowledge of the letter/sound (phoneme/grapheme) association and of spelling patterns.

Tests purporting to assess these various aspects of auditory functioning are *The Wepman Auditory Discrimination Test* (1958), revised edition (1973), the auditory sections of the *Illinois Test of Psycholinguistic Abilities* (Kirk, McCarthy and Kirk, 1968), *The Auditory Analysis Test* (Rosner and Simon, 1970), *The Screening Test of Auditory Perception* (Kimmel and Wahl, 1969), *The Auditory-Visual Pattern Test* (Birch and Belmont, 1965), *The Roswell-Chall Auditory Blending Test* (1963), *The Lindamood Auditory Conceptualization Test* (1971) and the memory span tests adapted from the Stanford-Binet (1960) and Wechsler Scales (1949). A full evaluation of these tests is contained in Barr (1972). Although all these tests have their value, it is felt that it is too time consuming to administer a different test for each aspect and, further, that none are sufficiently discerning in the areas requiring investigation to provide the necessary information for diagnosis and remediation in the light of current knowledge of specific learning difficulties, or indeed, the acquisition of reading and spelling in all children. The current thought on difficulties with spelling has been shown to be an inability to make, or lack of knowledge of making, the appropriate sound to symbol association (Snowling 1986).

The Hornsby Test, then, brings together an evaluation of the skills of auditory perception, phonemic segmentation, auditory memory and orthographic knowledge. These are the skills children need if they are to partake fully and successfully in school tasks, particularly where copying from the board, taking notes and writing stories and essays is concerned.

The need for the inclusion of intrapersonal as well as inter-personal speech monitoring has long been recognised by speech therapists, since children are usually very well able to detect articulation defects in others, but are often unable to discern the same mistakes when made by themselves—Marcel (1980), Carrell (1954), (1966), (1980). Kornfeld (1974) cites the example of the following conversation:

Adult: (*pointing to picture of rabbit*) 'What's that?'
Child: 'That's a /wabɪt/.'
Adult: 'No, say /rabɪt/, not /wabɪt/.'
Child: 'But I didn't say /wabɪt/, I said /wabɪt/.'

Marcel (1980) maintains that the imperfect monitoring of one's own speech code arises from the inability to distinguish certain features in personal speech which can be distinguished in the speech of others. While it is true that speech acquisition depends on the ability to perceive the distinctive features of speech sounds in order to comprehend and then to produce speech by translating this perceptual knowledge into motor programmes, it is unclear whether the monitoring of one's own speech production is entirely an auditory perceptual process. Certainly, it involves primarily bone conduction as well as air conduction, but also kinaesthetic feedback from the articulatory musculature. It must also involve auditory and proprioceptive memory for accurate programmes to be retained as referrents against which hypotheses can be tested.

Since writing is an even more complex activity than speech, involving the conversion of strings of phonemes to strings of letters (Hotopf 1980), it is to be expected that writing will prove a more difficult task than discriminating between pairs of words, particularly for the child whose pronunciation is faulty. The perception, repetition and proprioception involved in this test not only requires cross modal transference, but also the ability to set up a linguistic programme to realise what one has heard and kinaesthetically felt in written form, a process which puts short term memory at a premium. Ehri (1980) states that the ability to form orthographic images has important cognitive functions facilitating verbal memory and affecting the pronunciation of words. The ability to form orthographic images as symbols for sounds was found to emerge during the first two years of reading instruction and was among the capabilities distinguishing beginning readers who had acquired a large repertoire of printed words from those who had not. The phoneme to grapheme conversion has often been cited as lying at the heart of the disabled reader and speller's difficulties (Vernon 1971, Frith 1978). However, more important still in the acquisition of both spoken and written language is the laying down of sensory-motor patterns (kinaesthesis) which are considered by Lisker *et al.* (1962) to be as significant as the development of auditory perception when learning language. Written language, however, requires more than auditory perceptual or visual perceptual skills and kinaesthetic motor patterning. It requires the transference of all these abilities into writing, which again requires a knowledge of the orthographic representation of the English language. Thus, transcription skills of words correctly perceived as 'same' or 'different' will depend on *spelling ability* rather than *chronological age*, a finding substantiated by Snowling (1981), Frith (1978) and Nelson (1980).

Consonants require three distinctive features to be perceived at cortical level before they can be recognised and discriminations made between them:

1   *Manner*—how the sound is made.
2   *Place*—where the sound is made.
3   *Voicing*—whether there is vocal cord vibration or not.

The following difficulties in feature analysis have been clinically observed to occur most often and have, therefore, been incorporated in the word pairs of the test:

1   The confusion between the voiceless labio-dental and inter-dental fricatives /f/ and /θ/ (voiceless 'th') as in 'thin/fin'. This substitution is often present in children with reading and spelling difficulties regardless of social class or environmental influence.
2   The substitution of the voiced labio-dental and voiced fricatives /v/ and /ð/ (voiced 'TH') as in 'van/than'. Both the above are often reflected in the spelling 'wiv' for 'with', for example.

3   The confusion between the voiceless labio-dental fricative /f/ and the voiced labio-dental fricative /v/ as in 'off/of'. All the above differences have been found to be the most difficult to perceive, discriminate between and reproduce, both in speech and writing, and are among the last sounds to be acquired in speech.

4   The omission in spelling of the nasals /m/ and /n/ before a final voiceless stop consonant, as in 'lip/limp' and 'wet/went'. There have been many experiments regarding this aspect. Fujimura (1975) found that terminal nasal clusters on spectographic records showed that with a voiced stop ('tend') there was a distinct segmental realisation of the nasal, but with voiceless stops and affricates there was not. Marcel (1980) and Peters (1970) have produced similar findings. This is because the articulatory demands of voiceless stops /p/ /t/ /k/ and the affricate /tʃ/ (ch) are in conflict with those of a nasal. In order to accumulate the necessary air pressure which will identify a voiceless stop on release, the velum must close after the realisation of the nasal. For voiceless stops, affricates and fricatives preceded by a nasal, the velum remains open for a shorter segment of time during the realisation of the nasal. Further, the duration of vowels is longer before voiced stops so the nasalisation of the vowel before a final voiced consonant is more obvious. However, perception and repetition of word pairs in which the only phonemic difference is the inclusion or omission of a nasal, ('lip/limp', 'wet/went'), has not proved a problem with either normal readers or retarded readers. It is only at the transference level of sound to symbol that the system sometimes breaks down. Also, while trying to decide the nature of the difference the original stimulus is often lost to memory.

5   The confusion between the plosives b/d and p/b. Since these are mainly visual misconceptions they are seldom confused at the auditory discrimination level, but are common in the writing of children with specific spelling difficulty (Orton 1937), as in 'bad/dad' and 'prick/brick'.

6   The substitution of the voiced for voiceless alveolar plosives /d/ /t/ or the velar plosives /g/ /k/ as in 'bed/bet', 'got/cot'.

7   The confusion between the labio-nasal and alveolar nasal continuants /m/ and /n/ in the final position, as in 'then/them'.

8   The confusion between the voiceless velar plosive and the voiceless alveolar plosive /k/ /t/ as in 'lock/lot'.

9   The confusion between the liquids /l/ and /r/ in consonantal

clusters with preceding voiceless plosives, as in 'clam/cram'. The difficulty here involves the onset of voicing and, as with nasals, is more common with voiceless than with voiced consonants (Gimson 1972; Marcel 1980).

10 The confusion between the bilabial and post-alveolar friction-less continuants /w/ and /r/, as in 'wing/ring'. Young children commonly reproduce the post-alveolar /r/ first as bilabial /w/ and later as labio-dental. If these immaturities persist, substitution may occur in spelling.

Test Construction

The Nature of the Test

It has been found suitable for use with children from five to 15 years. However, with the very young child it may only be possible to give it as a test of auditory discrimination and accurate repetition task. If the *spelling age* is less than five years but the child can write 25 to 26 letters of the alphabet *to dictation*, the additional short vowel test only may be given for transcription.

It will be seen that all words on the list are within the spelling competence of children with a spelling age of five to nine years as measured on the Daniels and Diack (1974) Graded Spelling Test or the Schonell (1970) Graded Word Spelling Test.

In addition to the discrimination and spelling difficulties already mentioned, three pairs of words have been included specifically to detect a child with a high frequency hearing loss. These involve the sounds /f/ and /s/, which are presented in the initial and final positions: 'moth/moss', and 'sun/fun'. It is true that /f/ and /θ/ are also high frequency sounds, but these are very commonly confused even by children without hearing loss whereas /f/ and /s/ are not. By implication, as well as investigation, it is assumed that the former is mainly a cortical perceptual deficit while the latter indicates a peripheral hearing loss.

The Selection of Word Pairs

It was decided to use real words rather than non-words in spite of the difficulty in obtaining suitable pairs containing the oppositions /f/ /θ/; /v/ /ð/; /f/ and /v/. However, wherever possible words were kept within the AA and A frequency counts of the Thorndike Lorge Teacher's Word List (1963).

By using real words it is possible to relate the task to a child's spelling difficulties and pinpoint areas needing remediation.

As the test involves spelling as well as perceptual and discriminative tasks, the words are all one-syllable, phonetically regular words with only the five short vowels in them. The pairs of words that are different only differ by one phoneme (or sound). Fifteen pairs are 'different' and five are false choices—'the same'—to avoid patterning.

Nevertheless, the five 'same' pairs contain spelling subtleties such as knowledge of consonant blends and digraphs so that they can be meaningfully used in the transcription score.

Vowels are less often misperceived than consonants, so the phoneme changes all involved consonants. However, short vowels do sometimes present problems, so an additional short vowel test is included on the scoring sheet (p. 217), to be used if the need becomes apparent, or if the child's spelling age is insufficient for all word pairs to be transcribed.

Scoring

If the words are correctly repeated, place a tick in the R column. If the words are incorrectly repeated, place a cross in the R column and record exactly what the child has said in the 'Transcription spoken' space. *Only enter errors* in this column. This will not only give information about perceptual and production skills but will also highlight any speech defects.

If the short vowel test is given, place tick or cross in V column.

Count as correct words that have been accurately repeated but make a note if the order of the words has been reversed.

If the pair is correctly identified as different, place a tick in the D column.

If the pair is incorrectly identified as same, place a cross in the D column.

If the pair is correctly identified as same, place a tick in the S column.

If the pair is incorrectly identified as different, place a cross in the S column.

Place a tick in the W column if the pairs have been written correctly and *do not* write anything in the 'Transcription written' column. *Only record errors*.

Place a cross in the W column if the pairs have been written incorrectly and record the child's effort in the 'Transcription written' column.

Place a dash in the W column if a child is unable to attempt any given word. Transfer sum of scores in each column to appropriate box at bottom of record form. Count as correct any pair where the phonemic difference has been appreciated and the word has an acceptable phonetic spelling, but record the words for the purpose of suggesting areas of remediation. The quality of the child's phonic skills will also provide clues to teaching techniques required.

Examples of spelling that should be counted as correct, but recorded for diagnostic information:

'cut/cut' spelt 'kut/kut'

'moth/moss' spelt 'moth/mos'

Test Word Lists

	Word pairs	Same/ different	Content
1	lip/limp	different	/m/ before /p/, vowel /ĭ/
2	cut/cut	same	orthographic knowledge of initial /k/ sound, vowel /ŭ/
3	bad/dad	different	initial b/d, vowel /ă/
4	thin/fin	different	/th/ versus /f/, vowel /ĭ/
5	pat/pat	same	realisation of final /t/, vowel /ă/
6	prick/brick	different	discrimination of initial /p/ /b/ in consonantal clusters —vowel /ĭ/
7	bed/bet	different	final /d/ /t/, vowel /ĕ/
8	van/than	different	initial /v/ /th/, vowel /ă/
9	got/cot	different	initial /g/ /k/, vowel /ŏ/
10	wet/went	different	/n/ before /t/, vowel /ĕ/
11	rush/rush	same	knowledge of digraph /sh/, vowel /ŭ/
12	much/much	same	knowledge of digraph /ch/, vowel /ŭ/
13	off/of	different	final /f/ /v/ and knowledge of spelling, vowel /ŏ/
14	yes/yes	same	knowledge of graphemic representation of 'y', vowel /ĕ/
15	then/them	different	final /n/ /m/, vowel /ĕ/
16	moth/moss	different	final /th/ /s/ high frequency sounds, vowel /ŏ/
17	lock/lot	different	final /k/ /t/, vowel /ŏ/
18	sun/fun	different	initial /s/ /f/ high frequency sounds, vowel /ŭ/
19	clam/cram	different	/l/ /r/ in consonant blend, vowel /ă/
20	wig/rig	different	initial /w/ /r/, vowel /ĭ/

Administration

The Hornsby Test
The child should not be able to see your lips in order to prevent lipreading. The most satisfactory way of achieving this is to stand behind the child once the nature of the task has been explained and you have satisfied yourself that the child has understood. In this way the subject can only use his ears and you can observe the child's written efforts. You will also know when to present the next pair and record all responses directly onto the form. Standing behind the child has been found to be less distressing than turning one's back or covering one's mouth, but it should be explained that you are standing behind him because you want him only to use his ears.

Instructions to Subject
If the child cannot attempt any of the written transcriptions, this test is still useful as an auditory discrimination and oral repetition test. However, this does indicate that further formal teaching of letter/sound associations and their blending into words is needed.

Say: 'I am going to say two words. They will either be the same words that I am saying twice or the words will be different. Now, what about this pair: "man/man"?' (Said at one-second intervals in a clear, even voice, well pronunciated.)

'Say the words.' Child repeats.

'Are they the same, or are they different?' Child responds.

'That's right, they are the same. Now what about "pat/pet"? Say the words.' Child repeats.

'Are they the same, or are they different?' Child responds.

'That's right, they are different.'

If the child does not appear to understand, continue with 'bag/bag', 'dig/dog', until you are satisfied that the child knows what to do and is at ease. Then continue thus:

'I am going to say two pairs of words like that and I want you to say them out loud and then tell me whether they are the same or different. Then I want you to write them down on your piece of paper here.' (Indicate where you wish him to write).

Move behind the child's chair with the record form attached to a clipboard or firm card, and with a pen or pencil to record responses.

'Before each pair of words I am going to say "Ready".'

Presentation
'Ready? "Lip/limp"—say the words. Same or different? Good, now write them.'

Encourage the child with 'Good, well done, do the best you can', or whatever seems appropriate.

'Ready? "Cut/cut"—say the words. Same or different? Now write them.'

Continue in this way until all 20 pairs have been completed. Naturally, if the child is responding without the necessity of prompting, simply say the words. The words may be repeated if requested, but a note should be made of how many pairs needed to be repeated and which ones.

Also record the oral responses if the child reverses the order of the words.

Interpretation

Age	Norm	
5–6 years	Errors	4
7–8 years	Errors	3
8–9 years and over	Errors	2

The above table represents the norms for the auditory discrimination test only.

Above the level of these norms the child or adult should be referred for an audiometric hearing test, particularly if the errors include confusions between the sounds /f/ and /s/.

If errors are more than eight the test is invalidated, as the child is either severely deaf or has failed to understand the nature of the test.

The interpretation of the written transcriptions is for diagnostic purposes only and is intended as a guide to remediation as well as an indication of the level of auditory memory for symbolic material and the ability to make a mental image of such material in order to hold it in mind long enough for the words to be transferred to paper.

A child of five years of age with average or above average intellectual level should be able to make a 75 per cent acceptable attempt at the written transcription.

A child of six years of age with comparable intelligence should manage 90 per cent of the written words.

Acceptable responses would include such spellings as 'kut/cut'.

Scoring Sheet

Pre-test items   Man—Man ☐ Pat—Pet ☐ Bag—Bag ☐ Dig—Dog ☐

Hornsby Auditory Discrimination and Cross Modal Transference Test

	R	D	S	W	Transcription (spoken)	Transcription (written)	
1 lip—limp							Particulars of Subject
2 cut—cut							Name
3 bad—dad							d.o.b.
4 thin—fin							Age
5 pat—pat							I.Q.
6 prick—brick							Spelling age
7 bed—bet							Address
8 van—than							
9 got—cot							School
10 wet—went							
11 rush—rush							Date tested
12 much—much							Examiner
13 off—of							
14 yes—yes							SHORT VOWEL TEST
15 then—them							V Score
16 moth—moss							1 bit—bet
17 lock—lot							2 bet—bat
18 sun—fun							3 bat—but
19 clam—cram							4 cut—cot
20 wig—rig							5 cot—cat

TRANSCRIBE ERRORS ONLY

R	D	S	W	V
20	15	5	20	5
Repetition of spoken words	Pairs that are different	Pairs that are the same	Written pairs	Vowels

Other tests

Notes

References

BARR, D. F. (1972). *Auditory Perceptual Disorders*. Illinois: Charles Thomas.

BELMONT, I., BIRCH, H. G. and KARP, E. (1965). 'The disordering of sensory integration by brain damage'. *Nerv. Ment. Dis.* 141: pp. 410–418.

CARRELL, J. A. and Prendergast, K. (1954). 'An experimental of the possible relation between errors of speech and spelling. *J. of Speech and Hearing Disorders*, 19, pp. 327–334.

CARRELL, J. A. (1966). *Disorders of Articulation*. London: Prentice-Hall.

CARRELL, J. A. (1980). 'Pedogogic value of spelling tests', in Frith, U. (Ed.) *Cognitive Processes in Spelling*. London: Academic Press.

DANIELS, J. C. and DIACK, HUNTER (1973). *The Standard Reading Tests*. London: Chatto & Windus.

EHRI, L. G. (1980). 'The development of orthographic images', in Frith, U. (Ed.) *Cognitive Processes in Spelling*. London: Academic Press.

FRITH, U. (1976). 'How to read without knowing how to spell'. Paper presented to the British Association for Advancement of Science. University of Lancaster.

FRITH, U. (1980). *Cognitive Processes in Spelling*. (Ed.) London: Academic Press.

GRIMSON, A. C. (1970). *An Introduction to the Pronunciation of English*. London: Edward Arnold. 2nd Ed.

HENDERSON, L. and CHARD, M. J. (1978). *Word Recognition*. Final Report to the Social Science Research Council on grant No. H.R. 3301.

HOTOPF, N. (1980). 'Slips of the pen', in Frith, U. (Ed.) *Cognitive Processes in Spelling*. London: Academic Press.

KIMMELL, G. M. and WAHL, J. (1969). *The STAP Screening Test for Auditory Perception*. San Rafael: Academic Therapy Publications.

KIRK, S. A. and KIRK, W. D. (1970). *Psycholinguistic Learning Disabilities, Diagnosis and Remediation*. Chicago: University of Illinois Press.

KORNFELD, J. R. and GOEHL, H. (1974). 'A new twist to an old observation: kids know more than they say'. *Proceedings of the 10th Annual Meeting of the Chicago Linguistics Society*. Univ. of Chicago.

LINDAMOOD, C. and LINDAMOOD, P. (1970). *L.A.C. Test* (Lindamood Auditory Conceptualization Test). Boston: Teaching Resources.

LISKER, L., COOPER, F., and LIBERMAN, A. M. (1962). 'The uses of experiment in language description'. *Word*. 18: pp. 82–106.

MARCEL, A. J. (1980). 'Phonological awareness', in Frith, U. (Ed.) *Cognitive Processes in Spelling*. London: Academic Press.

NELSON, H. E. (1978). 'Spelling development and memory in childhood dyslexia'. PhD Thesis. London University.

ROSNER, J. and SIMON. D. (1970). *The Auditory Analysis Test: An Initial Report*. Pittsburgh Learning Research and Developmental Center, University of Pittsburgh.

ROSWELL, F. G. and CHALL, J. S. (1963). *Auditory Blending Test*. New York: Essay Press.

SCHONELL, F. J. and SCHONELL, F. E. (1956). *Diagnostic and Attainment Testing*. Edinburgh: Oliver & Boyd. 3rd Ed.

SNOWLING, M. 'The development of grapheme-phoneme correspondences in normal and dyslexic readers'. *J. of Exper. Child. Psychology*.

TERMAN, L. M. and MERRILL, M. A. (1960). *Stanford—Binet Intelligence Scale: Manual for the third revision, form L–M*. Boston: Houghton Mifflin.

VERNON, M. D. (1971). *Reading and its Difficulties*. London: Cambridge University Press.

WECHSLER, D. (1944). *The Measurement of Adult Intelligence*. Baltimore: Williams & Wilkins Co.

WEPMAN, J. M. (1973). *Auditory Discrimination Test*. University of Chicago PhD.

TIZARD, B. (1988). *Young Children in the Inner City*.

INDEX